THE CHALLENGE OF RELIGION AFTER MODERNITY

If God has departed, as Baudrillard claims, is religion still relevant? A new religious landscape is appearing in the new millennium. The middle classes with their electronic technologies are producing a culture of commodified images and signs that is radically transforming the religious landscape and re-enchanting the world. Ecstatic experiences pervade the re-enchanted world. Both fundamentalism and the New Age movement promote the free flow of charisma, reshaping religion in unforeseen directions.

Analysing the crisis of modernity, this book delves into the intricacies of these movements to examine the implications of religious change in the new millennium. The authors provide an incisive assessment of religious change in the West and Asia to suggest an eclecticism in re-enchantment that will usher in new ideas about charisma, consciousness and spirituality. These ideas focus on new forms of shamanism that point the way to experiences of empowerment beyond the structures of disenchantment.

I0887113

The Challenge of Religion after Modernity

Beyond disenchantment

RAYMOND L.M. LEE
SUSAN E. ACKERMAN

Routledge
Taylor & Francis Group
LONDON AND NEW YORK

First published 2002 by Ashgate Publishing

Reissued 2018 by Routledge
2 Park Square, Milton Park, Abingdon, Oxon OX14 4RN
711 Third Avenue, New York, NY 10017, USA

Routledge is an imprint of the Taylor & Francis Group, an informa business

A Library of Congress record exists under LC control number: 2002100836

ISBN 13: 978-1-138-73685-6 (hbk)
ISBN 13: 978-1-138-73680-1 (pbk)
ISBN 13: 978-1-315-18568-2 (ebk)

Contents

Preface

Religion was once believed to have taken a back seat as the world modernized. That no longer seems to be the case. Indeed, it has become more pronounced in a world marked by political upheavals, ethnic conflicts, economic uncertainties, ecological and gender crises. This is happening at a time of vast changes in communications, technology, politics and culture. It is this upsurge in religious activities around the world that has prompted us to ask the question, 'What is the future of religion in a world exhausted by the meaning of modernity?'.

To be modern is not to abandon religion, but to reorganize religion under the auspices of secular power. Secularization implies a process of social change that defines progress as an outcome of the rational mind and not the mystical transcendence of the phenomenal world. Yet, global religious revivalism represents efforts to challenge the secular outlook and to possibly restore charisma to spiritual pursuits.

Charisma is not a difficult word to understand if we conceptualize religious change in the new millennium as the reversibility of disenchantment. In the West, disenchantment has been the driving force of a distinct effort to seek total control of the external world. One could say that disenchantment was a form of totalitarianism for ridding the world of magic, superstition and arcane knowledge. Religion was not exempt from this totalitarian sweep of the once enchanted landscape. After the dust settled, enlightenment became another form of power play.

There are, however, signs of re-enchantment at the end of the twentieth century. The activities of the New Age movement and the yearning for ecstatic experiences in all types of new religion suggest that the limits of disenchantment have been reached. As we stand at the doorway between the Age of Reason and the New Age, religion is being reinvented as the return of charisma. Yet, it is important to ask how charisma is manifested in an emergent world of global markets and mass consumption. In this context of sweeping changes in economy and society, the interaction between the symbol and the sign becomes critical in understanding the re-enchantment of religion. The symbol has played a dominant role in various representations of the sacred, and it is almost unthinkable for many of us to talk about religion without the mediation of symbols. But, in the New Age, the sign replaces representation with revelry, a type of celebration of the senses that promotes bricolage, depthlessness and homogenization. The sign moulds re-enchantment into commodities of direct experiential power.

However, the symbol has not been completely overwhelmed by the sign. For example, religious fundamentalism is still spoken of as a symbol of intolerance and rigidity. Although traditional symbols continue to exercise influence over definitions of reality in many parts of the world the globalization of sign culture suggests that the struggle between symbols and signs has already begun.

It is not our intention to propose a semiotic theory of religious change. Our objective focuses on the meaning of post-Enlightenment religion in which re-enchantment signals the limits of bourgeois rationality and suggests alternative directions for mapping out the religious terrain of the new millennium. We want to show how the Enlightenment as a discourse of world mastery has been complicated by the effort to attain religious authenticity. In particular, the middle classes have ironically played an important role in reversing the quest for world mastery. Once the model of enlightened development, the middle classes are now being assailed by a postmodern sensibility that thrives on images, signs and the celebration of the market. This sensibility has provided the means for reinventing romanticism to re-enchant the world. Under the symbol, re-enchantment of the middle classes may take the form of fundamentalist beliefs and actions. On the other hand, signs of the New Age attract the middle classes to new trends in shamanism and dreaming. This comparison highlights once again the inevitable showdown between symbols and signs.

In our efforts to come to grips with the issues of class, self, power, charisma, and re-enchantment within a post-Enlightenment framework, we do not offer readers a neat theoretical statement of religious change in the new millennium. We address these issues to prompt further thinking on religious re-enchantment in the age of the sign. For helping us to bring our ideas to fruition, we would like to thank Sarah Lloyd and Elisabeth Arweck.

Chapter 1

Divinity after Modernity

For the last four centuries, the West had equated Enlightenment with the avenue to modern progress.[1] This was the enlightenment of mind over matter, the ability to call forth the powers of reason as a human mirror of divine perfection. Under the aegis of the Western Enlightenment, religion gradually took on the mantle of performative disbelief. Religion became an instrument of institutional growth rather than an end in itself. Yet as the twentieth century wore on, the realization that modernity did not engulf religion compelled people to question the wisdom of progress without eschatological meaning. Hence, the emergence of the New Age movement, the Western discovery of Eastern religions, the zest of neo-Pentecostalism, the revival of religion in post-communist societies, and the apparent rise of fundamentalism comprise significant events that suggest a radicalization of religion. Old and new gods, gurus and new religious movements compete vigorously for spiritual attention. Are we witnessing a trend towards the re-enchantment of the world? To answer this question, we need to explore the factors that have transformed the quest for world mastery into a revitalization and redefinition of sacred identity.

The Angst of World Mastery

The essence of the Western Enlightenment lies in the peculiar Western veneration for self-criticism. This is epitomized by Immanuel Kant's question of 1784 – '*Was ist Aufklärung?*' ('What is Enlightenment?'). He found the answer in the human ability for reflexive thought. Reflexivity in this case provided the premise to doubt as the pre-condition for liberation from traditional forms, ideas and practices. The flight from tradition, indeed, constitutes the unfolding of the Enlightenment as the abandonment of ancient and medieval thought forms. These forms allegedly held back the maturation of the doctrine of progress. Human bondage to these forms could only be broken by heavy doses of rationalism and empiricism. Thus, Western philosophers of the eighteenth century emphasized these two methods as the basis for distinguishing between faith and knowledge. They comprised the means for the determination of an objective truth, which was only possible through an uncompromising scepticism deeply implanted in human reflexivity.

The Western Enlightenment was, therefore, a grand project of emancipation. It was aimed at purifying human consciousness of centuries of superstition, mythologies and confusion. By addressing the self as the wellspring of reason and knowledge, it was believed that the universe would come into the service of humankind. In other words, the Enlightenment pointed the way to world mastery by excavating reason as the inexorable substitute for providence. World mastery came to be synonymous with the Enlightenment's purchase on science as the means for revealing ultimate truth. The philosophers of the Western Enlightenment did not initiate the scientific worldview, but they were instrumental in popularizing and utilizing it as a tool of social change.[2] They did not attribute social change to divinity, but to individuals endowed with rational powers for understanding the laws of their environment.

Max Weber perhaps provided, in the early part of the twentieth century, the most explicit statement on the transformation of Enlightenment science into an institution of world mastery.[3] For Weber, world mastery simply meant mastery of all things by calculation, which implied a process of disenchantment and the marginalization of magical means. Yet, science as a vocation, in Weber's opinion, could not provide decisive meanings about the universe. World mastery through scientific means offered to humankind a sense of self-determination, but it could not indefatigably replace the sacred values and revelations of the prophets.[4] This was a suggestion that the power of faith could not be fully broken in a world governed by the spirit of scepticism. Such a world could only exist within the bounds of abstraction, reification and domination – principles that empowered the human imagination but not its sense of salvation.

Abstraction is the foremost method by which consciousness is transformed into conceptual categories via language for the purpose of naming, confronting and manipulating a world 'out there'. It makes reality an ongoing concern because there is no dearth of external objects to be grasped and known. The intellectualization of the world based on abstraction makes possible the apprehension of diverse phenomena. It differentiates the world into multiple disciplines of understanding. It is this process that has made world mastery an exhilarating, but contentious, experience. Contention arises not from the myriad things in the world, but from the isolation of the self from the abstract structures of society. These are structures that have seemingly attained autonomy from their human creators. As Zijderveld puts it, 'modern man faces his society as a relatively autonomous reality to which he experiences but little correspondence'.[5]

From abstraction it is but a short step to reification or the process by which consciousness objectifies all experiences and perceptions as real – that is, existing on their own terms as though they are inherently independent and causal in nature. For Lukács, reification is dependent on the commoditization of everything in society and social relations acquire a 'phantom objectivity' – that is, 'an autonomy that seems so strictly rational and all-embracing as to conceal every trace of its fundamental nature'.[6] The development of scientific knowledge tends to result in a 'formally closed system of partial laws' that is unable to transcend its own boundaries.[7]

It is through this closed system that domination is exercised as a mandate of the rational self to identify and control all the objects of the external world for the alleged benefit of humankind. World mastery is not just a matter of conceptual systematization, but the application of such a system within the language of its operation to the practical demands of everyday life. Hence, domination is the control and manipulation of a conventional reality deemed accessible to human interpretation and understanding. But this is an understanding based on awe and fear of nature. Since the time of Bacon, this understanding has provided the motive for humans to rule over nature as part of the belief in a divinely inspired plan.[8]

The principles of abstraction, reification and domination worked well only under the spirit of scepticism. This spirit seemingly provided the means for achieving clarity of thought, discriminating perception and unbiased knowledge. It allegedly cleared the path between superstition and science, tradition and inquiry, ignorance and enlightenment. Since the advent of Cartesian doubt, the sceptical element in the Western Enlightenment has been primarily responsible for charting all the possibilities of modernity. The age of world mastery can be said to be a distillation of methodical scepticism suffusing the principles of abstraction, reification and domination to the point that the original belief in divine inspiration became overshadowed by the hubris of a wanton self-determinism. Yet, it is this same scepticism that has in recent decades cut its connections to the rational mechanisms of the Enlightenment project. It has also brought forth the view that the Enlightenment is not a predestined palliative for the human condition, but merely a project of immense contradiction.

The postwar publication of Horkheimer and Adorno's critique of the Enlightenment marks the beginning of the implosive effects of Western scepticism.[9] There is an antinomian thrust in this work because it attempts to show that Enlightenment morality is not binding on critics who are able to discern its contradictions. Horkheimer and Adorno dismissed the Western Enlightenment as a form of domination masquerading as self-determinism: 'Myth turns into enlightenment, and nature into mere objectivity. Men pay for the increase of their power with alienation from that over which they exercise their power. Enlightenment behaves toward things as a dictator toward men.'[10] They saw abstraction as merely a tool of Enlightenment and domination as its consequence. In the final analysis they argued that 'enlightenment is as totalitarian as any system'.[11] From this premise, they extrapolated the hegemonic characteristics of the Enlightenment to the cultural and political realms. In culture, they construed technological rationale as the rationale of domination:

> It is the coercive nature of society alienated from itself. Automobiles, bombs, and movies keep the whole thing together until their leveling element shows its

> strength in the very wrong which it furthered. It has made the technology of the culture industry no more than the achievement of standardization and mass production, sacrificing whatever involved a distinction between the logic of the work and that of the social system.[12]

Politically, anti-Semitism became an outgrowth of the institutions of domination fostered by the Enlightenment. Horkheimer and Adorno concluded that, 'race has become the self-assertion of the bourgeois individual integrated within a barbaric collectivity ... The persecution of the Jews, like any other form of persecution, is inseparable from that system of order'.[13]

In short, the age of world mastery had given birth to master institutions and master races. Modernity merely reflects the deepening of these institutions and ideologies in mass society. It is no wonder, then, that a postmodernist such as Zygmunt Bauman would treat modernity as a condition that made racism possible. In a rather perceptive statement, he suggested that because the Enlightenment fostered an engineering attitude towards the external world, racism could not be easily distinguished from other mundane activities such as gardening and medicine. These activities shared the same goal of identifying and exterminating 'harmful' elements from 'useful' ones.[14]

Bauman's critique provides a continuing link with that of Horkheimer and Adorno. Jürgen Habermas, on the other hand, seems less pessimistic about the Enlightenment project and is intent on rewriting its agenda as communicative action.[15] Communicative action resuscitates the Enlightenment project by offering hope that rests on the 'community forming and solidarity building force of unalienated cooperation and living together'.[16] The possibility of this utopian scenario rests on linguistic and cultural practices that result in mutual understanding and identity affirmation, thus providing the context and resources for the construction of meaning in the lifeworld as opposed to the instrumental rationality of the social system. Bowring summarizes this strategy of emancipation as 'the discursive redemption of normative validity claims'.[17]

This is clearly an attempt to halt the imploding effects of Western scepticism by invoking a pragmatic attitude towards social and cultural recovery. Communicative action, therefore, represents Habermas's attempt to rescue the meaning of the Enlightenment as an intersubjective understanding of truth produced by networks of trust that are embedded in linguistic and cultural norms. Enlightenment in this sense generates inclusive values for the purpose of establishing distinct identities between individual and community. Its viability can be construed as an outcome of the secularization process that has elevated the realm of the mundane above that of the sacred since the end of the medieval period in the West.

Secularization is an intensely debated term in the West.[18] One reason for this is that it has to do with the state of religious influences in everyday life.

Generally speaking, the term has come to mean the retreat of religion from all spheres of society. It implies the diminished role of divinity in the public and, to a certain extent, the private realm. Instead, individualistic rationalism has become the interior voice of human conscience and reflexivity. The sacred, on the other hand, has taken refuge in rituals conducted for the sake of appearance and cultural continuity. Yet, there is considerable debate on the usefulness of the term.[19] Therefore, it is necessary to see how the term has evolved and its present application in relation to the meaning of the Western Enlightenment.

The Latin root word *saeculum* refers to a great length of time or may even imply a satanic domination of the world. In the Middle Ages, it referred to priests serving in ordinary parishes as opposed to those in religious orders. By the seventeenth century it meant the transference of land from church to civil authorities. In the eighteenth century, when land transference became more political, the term came to denote conflict between church and civil authority. The association of secularization with militant atheism was accomplished by the nineteenth century.[20] In other words, secularization cannot be analysed as an autonomous term outside the social and historical context of Europe. It reflects the changing conditions of power in which the clerical structure of authority is undermined by emerging bourgeois institutions of knowledge, government and opinion.

The emergence of these institutions must be considered in relation to the meaning of the Christian *eskhaton* for the rising bourgeoisie.[21] The *eskhaton* was the conceptualization of the end of the world or the final state in salvationary expectations. In their rise to power, the bourgeoisie reduced the importance of the *eskhaton.* Its marginalization meant the possibility of addressing all activities in the here-and-now for immediate accomplishment. It fostered an ideology of 'presentism' that seeks only to treat mastery of the moment as critical for objective control and progress. This is the context in which the secular became synonymous with bourgeois creativity and dynamism. With these ideological changes, the eschatological state became an anachronism or an ambiguous belief that could be mothballed indefinitely.

Deferment of eschatology implies that the Enlightenment cannot logically be conceived as a vehicle for the salvation of the individual soul, but rather for its gratification in the matrix of shared social understanding. Enlightenment is, therefore, the secularized bourgeoisie's approach to using this deferment as 'borrowed time' for enhancing the faculty of reason in the interest of world construction and domination. There is an underlying hope that the deferment would be sublimated into an unprecedented level of human self-determinism and understanding without recourse to the anticipation of divine intervention. With the eschatological state no longer regarded as intrinsic to their well-being and survival, the bourgeoisie finds it unnecessary to be beholden to the clerics and men of God for religious inspiration, guidance and rule. Within the context of their rising power, the bourgeoisie is able to turn this deferment of eschatology into their own condition for exercising power over that of the clerical structure.

Hence, the secular has now come to connote the loss of clerical power. This is reflected in the contemporary definitions of the secular. Shiner, for instance, links the secular to the decline of religion; a shift from other-worldly to this-worldly orientations; the differentiation of religious ideas and institutions from other aspects of society; the transposition of religious beliefs and activities to non-religious systems of thought; the demystification or disenchantment of the world; and the movement from a closed to an open system of rationality.[22] Indeed, recent definitions of the term have become more refined to suggest a decline of religious authority rather than religion *per se*.[23]

These definitions stressing the erosion of institutional religion complement the ascendancy of religious scepticism as evidenced by the statistics on increasing public disengagement from the churches in Europe. In the United States, this trend is reinforced by the view that churches there have been transformed into secular institutions.[24] These data suggest that the world has entered an era of decreasing religious expectation. Although religious institutions continue to exist and play a role in everyday life, they are no longer held in awe or assigned special authority by the masses. Instead, religious expectation is replaced by a cultural expectation of generalized purposive interaction. This is the context that is celebrated by Habermas as the potential arena for reinvigorating the Enlightenment project. It is not the church that is seen as the sole arbiter of personal enlightenment, but the mass of rational individuals working in tandem to produce a collectivity of enlightenment.

Yet, Habermas has not considered the rise of new religious movements as a possible challenge to communicative rationality. These are movements that attempt to reintroduce a sense of eschatology to the masses. As suggested by Stark and Bainbridge, secularization is a self-limiting phenomenon that eventually results in religious reactions taking the form of revivals and cultic innovations.[25] Their argument is based on the assumption that disillusionment with traditional churches and religious institutions may not be a sign of the weakening of religion. Rather, people may turn to alternative religious worldviews for securing their faith in salvationary goals. In this situation of limited secularization, the communicative rationality of Habermas is confronted by the tensions between religious consciousness and the secularized environment.[26] These tensions cannot be easily resolved by communicative rationality because disenchantment in a secularized environment may in fact be fuelling the search for religious meaning. In short, the self-limiting nature of secularization suggests its own paradox: the institutionalization of world mastery on a grand scale inadvertently problematized the quest for meaning and provided a source for the development of new religious movements.[27] To understand this paradox, we need to examine the problem of reflexivity.

The Crisis of Reflexivity

The Western Enlightenment empowered reflexivity to place the subject at the centre of the lifeworld. The goals of world mastery could not be realized without the mediation of reflexivity. Only in reflexive thought could the empirical achievements of science and technology and all forms of materialistic endeavour converge to produce the kind of knowledge deemed vital for the manipulation of the external world. Yet, the reflexivity that is so vital to the emergence of new ideas and knowledge is itself a destabilizing force because no theory, viewpoint or paradigm can remain the same in the light of incessant rethinking.[28] Reflexivity produces multiple, competitive choices. The greater the range of choices generated from reflexive thought, the more likely it is for the subject to perceive a gradation of choices relative to his or her interests.

The crisis of subject-centred knowledge in the twentieth century is, therefore, the crisis of modern progress. The meaning of modern progress as the social construction of prosperity fulfilled by the power of reason has been turned on its head by the brutalities of the twentieth century: international wars, ethnic unrest, genocide, class inequalities, environmental degradation and reignited nationalism form a reflexive undertow on the grand achievements of science, technology, medicine and other humanistic endeavours. From the perspective of the subject, the centre cannot hold as long as the meaning of progress is perennially contradicted by the uncontrolled violence of its underside. Therefore, it is necessary for the subject to transform the meaning of progress into that of risks in order to maintain some purchase on the uncertainties of the present age.[29]

In religion, uncertainty has created a peculiar sense of panic. This is a panic concerning the failed anticipation in resolving the problem of evil – that is, the rationalization of evil as an existential enigma in relation to the idea of a benign and compassionate divinity. First, the problem of evil has been intensified by the brutalities of the twentieth century. From Hitler's 'Final Solution' to 'ethnic cleansing' in the Balkans in the 1990s, humankind's inhumanity increased awareness of the need for self-consciousness to overcome the passivity of divinity in dealing with the problem of human destructiveness. The clash between reflexivity and the problem of evil was inevitable. The greater good of humankind could not be assured by an eschatological reckoning based on the benign intercession of divinity. Under these circumstances, reflexivity constituted a self-generated response towards the need for more secular attempts in controlling destructive actions in the world. It used uncertainty as a guideline for constructing a sense of worth in the self-ability to conquer the heart of darkness. This meant that religion could not singly solve the problem of evil, but required a renewed participation of the self in actualizing the powers of the Enlightenment. Hence, uncertainty has ironically given a boost to the meaning of subjectivity.

This subjectivity was valorized by Western youth culture of the 1960s and 1970s. David Martin saw it as a desire to gain 'a total view of the world',[30] defined as an undifferentiated view linking one discipline with another, interweaving facts with desire, and celebrating the joys of relativity. In Martin's eyes, the total view underscored the ahistorical nature of youth consciousness, producing a hostile reaction to the historical character of Christianity. The morality embedded in Christian history was seen as contrary to the ideology of the unrestrained self in youth culture.[31] Hence, Christianity in the latter half of the twentieth century lost its grounding in the intellectual and salvationary tradition established over a period of almost two millennia. It could no longer stand on its own against the uncertainties of the human heart.

For Martin, Christianity faced 'indifference, magic, nationalism, liberalism, scientism and Marxism'.[32] Each of these 'isms' constituted a putative attempt at circumventing uncertainty. There was indeed greater confidence attributed to these attempts than to the singular role of Christianity in fulfilling its salvationary promises. In the end, Christianity had to forge alliances with the 'isms' of the secular world, as suggested by Martin, or develop a strategy that did not make the Gospel repulsive to the public. This latter strategy constituted an attempt to search for a preachable Gospel. Particularly in the case of Britain, Gilbert noted that in 1963 the 'Honest to God' debate represented such an attempt, which only made it vacuous and provided no compelling reason to bring people back to church.[33]

In other words, Christianity failed to maintain a plausible account of the problem of evil and its solution. It could not effectively fend off the challenges of reflexivity and human agency. At a time when the world was becoming gruesomely destructive and distant, human agency was considered all the more pertinent to the amelioration of conflicts. Religious views and programmes centred on human agency were deemed vital to combat the pessimism developing from the uncertainty of one's station in life. For this reason, liberation theology developed in Latin America as a subjective reaction to the failure of the church to secure release of the impoverished from the uncertainty of their immediate circumstances. Liberation theology revitalized the notion that the poor were as much agents of history as their oppressors; they were not to be regarded as passive recipients of institutional charity. Löwy emphasized that liberationist Christianity in Latin America was a special instance of reflexivity based on the deprivations arising from economic dependency and the elation of revolutionary movements. For him:

> the formation of liberationist Christianity did not start, top-down, from the upper reaches of the Church … nor from bottom-up … but from the periphery to the centre [because] … the driving force of renewal [was] all, in one way or another, marginal or peripheral in relation to the institution: lay movements and their advisers, lay experts, foreign priests, religious orders.[34]

These developments in Latin America suggest that reflexive action, particularly from the periphery, restored a sense of subjective control over the lifeworld of the underprivileged. Even in an impoverished state, the subject understood that he or she was as much the centre as his or her tormentors. The church lost the status of centre because it was seen to be merely a bearer of dogma rather than an activator of agency. David Martin's impressive study of evangelical Protestantism in Latin America showed that, aside from the influences of liberation theology, the subject sought renewal in the comfort of Pentecostal activities. He or she rejected the vast impersonal structures of the church in order to find within him or herself the power to ascertain the meaning of spiritual development and solidarity. This power represented the dynamism of agency in breaking away from the traditional Catholic Church.[35]

These studies suggest that the subject's personal experiences in self-renewal constitute a form of reflexivity directed at questioning institutions and their ideologies. The meaning of salvation is not construed as a *sine qua non* of organizational membership but of individual decision based on personal choice. Reflexivity produced a highly self-conscious discourse on the institutional effects of religion, while turning these effects into a motive for seeking alternative forms of spiritual liberation. Thus, religious renewals in the West could be conceived as attempts to break through institutional constraints by reversing the contents of secularized consciousness into an exploration of inner personal experiences. Nowhere was this exploration more intense than in the Western rediscovery of the esoteric.

The Appeal of Esotericism

It seems contradictory to say that modernity provides a secret path to esotericism, but the paradox of secularization suggests that this is not impossible. The esoteric approach to enlightenment differs from the Enlightenment underlying modern consciousness. It is an inner change in awareness that takes its cue from the restrictions of modern knowledge and practice. Enlightenment that is derived from esotericism is concerned with the nature of undifferentiated experience, which constitutes the outcome of the pursuit of hidden knowledge astutely guarded by special individuals. This knowledge, as Tiryakian puts it, 'is of a participatory sort, namely, a knowledge (or gnosis) of the meaning of the world to human existence, in the progressive realization of which the subject develops internally and liberates himself from the strictures of everyday life'.[36]

Concealment is, therefore, a major characteristic of esoteric knowledge because such knowledge has the propensity to be misunderstood by ordinary people. Modern knowledge, on the other hand, is thought to be more accessible to the general public because it is deemed vital for survival and world mastery. Yet, we witness a gradual reversal of these characteristics as the new millennium unfolds. Esoteric knowledge is becoming more available to the seekers of the New Age.[37] Modern knowledge is ironically becoming more exclusive as increased differentiation in the technological, economic, social and cultural fields erects more barriers to general understanding. Increased differentiation in these fields adds complexities to the secularization of the environment. New structures appear and develop at a rapid rate, giving the impression that what is known and practised today becomes obsolete by tomorrow. No one person is able to have at his or her command the breadth of knowledge for comprehending changes in all these fields.

These developments contribute to the fragmentation of secularized consciousness. The perception and cognition of objects in the secularized fields tend to lose their sense of unity. The assumed correspondence between identity and knowledge is no longer taken at face value. An outcome is the alienation of knowing from meaning. Knowledge in each field or subfield becomes the basis for the emergence of specific norms, values and practices. Linkages between fields and subfields tend to become more tenuous. Consequently, the instrumentality of knowledge dominates the operations and activities of each field or subfield, and questions concerning the purpose of knowledge become peripheral. The fragmentation of secularized consciousness is, therefore, a movement towards multiple identities geared to the development of expertise in fields or subfields, all seemingly driven by the need to achieve world mastery rather than by questions of ultimacy.

The demand for esoteric knowledge intensifies as the limits to multiple identities are reached. These are limits that define the aridity of field and subfield expertise, the poverty of empirical knowledge for world mastery, and the inadequacies of hegemonic divisions and orientations. In his study of the revival of occultism in the West, Tiryakian argued that the particular appeal of esoteric knowledge could be attributed to 'a loss of confidence in established symbols and cognitive models of reality, in the exhaustion of institutionalized collective symbols of identity'.[38] His critical argument is that esoteric culture is not fundamentally distinct from modern culture. Both cultures share many similar referents from religious texts and figures to doctrines on dialectical materialism. Yet, modernization as an aspect of the bourgeois revolution has advanced values based on rationalism, industrialism and the scientific ethos over those based on the gnostic approaches of esoteric culture. Even though esoteric knowledge has been marginalized, it continues to make itself felt through countercultural movements against bourgeois values, particularly those inspired by romanticism.[39]

In other words, the continuous secularization of consciousness has produced an illusory sense of freedom through the creation of multiple identities in a rationalized social order. The loss of meaning reflects the failure of modern culture in maintaining this sense of freedom as real and lasting. It has led to a crisis of modern knowledge – should the knowledge and practices for the accomplishment of world mastery be abandoned because they are considered shallow, or salvaged because there are no better alternatives? Yet, the reappearance of esoteric knowledge in this crisis cannot effectively displace the structures of the secularized environment because the cultural, economic and political interests associated with these structures have become hegemonic. These interests define the conditions of everyday life and resist the intrusion of esotericism into their arenas of operation and production. Resistance may take the form of concerted action against new religious movements and cults,[40] or channel definitions of the esoteric into the realms of fantasy for mass entertainment such as in movies, video games, science fiction and so on. But the transformation of secularized consciousness into a search for significant inner experiences has initiated an exploration and utilization of secularized structures for the purpose of advancing the goals of esoteric enlightenment. The rise of Western Buddhism offers an example of such transformation.

Even though Buddhism in the West is still a minority religion, its growth since the end of the Second World War has been phenomenal. In the United States, about 1.6 per cent (3–4 million people) of the population is Buddhist. Of this number, about 800 000 are Euro-American Buddhists. In France 1.15 per cent (650 000 people) of the population has been identified as Buddhist. About 150 000 of the French Buddhists are ethnic Europeans. Smaller communities of Buddhists are found in Europe from Britain to Russia, generally not exceeding 1 per cent of the population.[41] For an Asian religion that was recently transplanted in the West, these figures signal an important development in Western receptivity to the search for an alternative form of enlightenment. Buddhist enlightenment is esoteric in the sense that it is concerned with the inner realization of perfect knowledge. The accomplishment of this goal requires a meditative shift towards the cultivation of inner equanimity.

The United States leads in the Western adoption of Buddhism as providing an esoteric path to the attainment of enlightenment. There are 500 to 800 Buddhist centres in the United States[42] which is also home to many leading Buddhist practitioners, scholars and publishers. In a perceptive survey of American Buddhism, Tamney remarked that:

> Buddhism is now part of American culture. An aura of exoticism has been lost. A certain acceptance, at least among educated people, has been gained.... Naturally, Americans interested in Buddhism have tended to be those who are repelled by Christianity.... The cross, the pope, and 'the Book' are, for some, profoundly disquieting religious symbols. In contrast, Buddhism does not associate nature with 'lower,' has no dogma, and simply asks potential converts to experience Buddhism.[43]

For Tamney, the critical reason for American receptivity to Buddhism was the need to escape from modernity. He saw this as a partial response to 'the felt loss of valuable aspects of the preindustrial world.... Remnants of a lost world have been found in Buddhist philosophy, in Buddhist communes, and in the image of the Buddha.'[44]

The pursuit of esoteric enlightenment, at least for American Buddhists, suggests a loss of confidence in the expectations of secularized consciousness. American Buddhists attempt to transcend secularized consciousness in order to attain alternative levels of awareness. However, this is not an attempt that includes a rejection of the secularized environment. American Buddhists perceive the institutional forms of the secularized environment as the appropriate conduits for the dissemination of Buddhist teachings and practices. In Lopez's study of the influence of Tibetan Buddhism in the West, he showed specifically how its intellectual development in America occurred through the secular institutions of higher learning and publishing outlets that represented the secular trust in print culture. He concluded by saying: 'The products of [Tibetan] monasteries were now teaching in the classrooms of American universities and graduate students were memorizing the formulas of their theology.'[45] Buddhism in contemporary American society, therefore, presents a unique example of the attenuation of secularized consciousness within the institutions of a highly secularized environment. This emergent situation has made possible the dissemination of esoteric knowledge, once considered secret and reserved for the attention of a select few, to Western Buddhists striving for inner realization.

Esoteric Buddhist texts and rituals have caught the attention of the Western public. For example, the English translation of esoteric texts such as the *Tibetan Book of the Dead* or *Bardo Thödol* is available to anyone who is interested in this type of knowledge. The *Bardo Thödol* is believed to be a hidden text produced by an Indian sage named Padmasambhava in the eighth century and discovered in the fourteenth century by Karma Lingpa, a Tibetan lama. It provides an in-depth description of the death experience and suggests techniques for transcending that experience in order to attain inner enlightenment.[46] Esoteric teachings on consciousness transference are also available to the public. For example, the Tibetan Buddhist technique of *phowa* or the transference of consciousness at the moment of death has been taught openly to the public.[47]

A certain degree of romanticism underlies the receptivity to and pursuit of esoteric knowledge by Western Buddhists. Western Buddhism is romantically driven because it offers a form of holistic recovery of the self through an acquisition of esoteric knowledge and techniques in a highly secularized environment that produces fragmented identities. In a context of high secularization, Buddhism provides an important alternative because it is a philosophy and practice of reversing world mastery. Its appeal in the West is unlikely to wane because the doubts and ambivalence of secularized consciousness are gradually transforming the path of disenchantment into that of re-enchantment.

Signs of Re-enchantment

Religion once symbolized the integrative forces of tradition. The Western Enlightenment elevated the power of reason above that of religion, challenging the legitimacy of religion as a system of salvation. Consequently, religion was redefined as a possible source of instability in societies that were reorganizing their values for industrial and secular development. This is the contemporary meaning of religion adumbrated by Beckford who wrote:

> Religion has come to represent a source of disorder in a world increasingly dominated by advanced industrial societies.... Accordingly, religion is coming to be seen as either a direct threat to the prevailing order, an indirect challenge to its constitutive values, or a declining source of social integration.[48]

But in the second half of the twentieth century, the crisis of modernity opened up new fields of religious experiences linked to the esoteric. It produced a zest for novel experiences in meditation, shamanism, ritual performances and healing. Indeed, sociologists of religion had to invent a new field of research to cope with expanding choices in unconventional religions.[49] Discovery of new religious experiences and fields of research can be interpreted as an indication of a growing trend towards the re-enchantment of the world. It is a trend that disprivileges the authority of the rational and renews understanding of the irrational. In a sense, re-enchantment is the very opposite of disenchantment. It is, as Tiryakian asserts, 'a major counterprocess of modernity',[50] having strong roots in the Romantic Movement of the eighteenth and nineteenth centuries. The thrust of re-enchantment is to negate the disparagement of magical power by the forces of secularization. Repression of the irrational by advocates of the Enlightenment no longer seems to work in an era where romanticism has found new life in many religious cults and movements. In seeking emancipation from the oppression of secularized society, many individuals found sources of re-enchantment in Asian religions (such as Buddhism, Hinduism and Taoism), neo-paganism and varieties of mysticism. Re-enchantment restored the primordial power that was allegedly lost or concealed in the drive towards modernity.

The beneficiaries of re-enchantment were individuals whose identities were sharply affected by the crisis of modernity. Their experiences of the desolate landscape of modernity drove them to experiment with esoteric forms of religious consciousness. In particular, many individuals from the middle classes sought refuge in new religious activities because it was in these classes that the aporias of modernity were most keenly felt. The prosperity and comfort enjoyed by members of the middle classes were derived from their central role in the processes of modernization. Yet, it was these same individuals who rebelled against disenchanted bourgeois values by embarking on a sojourn of re-enchantment. For example, Wuthnow observed that religious experimentation in American society was facilitated by relatively high levels of education and economic prosperity.[51] Alienation of the middle classes, therefore, constitutes an important factor in the trend towards re-enchantment (to be discussed in Chapter 3).

The role of the modern bourgeoisie in the re-enchantment of the world cannot be separated from the processes of signification that are occurring in late capitalism. These are processes involving the authentication of reality through the interaction of symbols and signs. In late capitalism, rationalization has developed to a point of gilding all production with efficiency and predictability that level, as well as mesmerize, the expectations of individual consumers. The transformation of the assembly line into a cornucopia of unfulfilled desires represents the grand achievement of late capitalist rationalization. George Ritzer used the term 'McDonaldization' to capture the illusion of freedom perpetuated by late capitalist strategies of resource mobilization, marketing and management.[52] It is in the McDonaldization of society that re-enchantment is occurring under the influence of signs rather than symbols. In other words, the middle-class search for new religious meaning is not merely a reaction to modernity, but an exploration of the esoteric in a context dominated by signs.

The sign differs from the symbol in the sense that the symbol represents something, whereas the sign is its own reality devoid of representation. A sign resembles a code for simplifying a particular mental operation, but as it develops into an elaborate pattern it acquires its own sense of structure. This is a second-order structure that stands above the original codes or symbols. In Gottdiener's study of Western mass culture, he argued that objects that possess user and exchange values eventually pass through market processes to attain sign value.[53] In simple terms, objects used in everyday life are transformed into signs by social groups producing subcultural codes. Similarly, mass culture producers take the personalized objects of subcultures and turn them into commercialized signs. These signs have lives of their own. They do not exist outside a self-referential system.

In modernity, the differentiation of social and cultural spheres has led to symbolic diversification. Symbolic meanings become self-contained in individual spheres. Each sphere appears to generate its own symbolic codes that do not necessarily correspond to those in other spheres. Communication between spheres is complicated by differences in symbolic codes arising from systemic differentiation. However, the translation of meaning across differentiated spheres is accomplished by the development of a sign system that stands above the symbolic meanings in each sphere. Signs generate a higher order of meaning that facilitates communication between spheres without the need to refer to the symbolic codes of individual spheres. They constitute an overarching system that can absorb and codify all the complexities of different social and cultural spheres. In highly secular market-oriented societies, money constitutes such a sign system. Money 'talks' because it represents its own reality in exchange relationships between spheres with different symbolic codes. Other signs are emerging in the wake of new cultural and technological developments. For instance, the advent of personal computers suggests that a sign system based on electronic simulation will come to dominate future social realities.[54]

In the McDonaldization of society, religious symbols are reorganized as signs to meet the growing demands and needs of consumers. As a sign, the symbolic god becomes equivalent to symbolic goods that are generalizable to a higher order of meaning. Whatever the word 'god' is made out to be, its meaning is no longer centred in the religious sphere but distributed in other spheres that collectively come under the domination of the sign. Thus, religious symbols are no longer representative of salvationary meanings in the traditional sense. Old symbols may be reactivated or mixed with other symbols to provide the self with new religious experiences. The self, having been cut loose from the symbolic stringency of the abstract god, is free to seek out other objects of worship revealed through alternative sources of re-enchantment. But the self does not necessarily develop and maintain long-lasting ties to these sources. As a consumer, the self merely uses and manipulates these sources for immediate experiential purposes. In this way, the self is drawn into the eclecticism and novelty of a system of salvationary signs.

In short, the sign rearranges the relationship of symbols into new forms of spiritual association that are not under the influence of religious institutions but the market forces of supply and demand. These forces reflect the trend in which religious actions are no longer dictated by ecclesiastical norms and decrees. The individual seeker is exposed to a wide range of choices in a market situation where signs compete for the attention of religious consumers. He or she becomes enmeshed in a vast network of images and messages that are consumed as commodities of salvation. The case of New Age shamanism (to be discussed in Chapter 5) provides an example of how traditional symbols of magical power are transformed in a system dominated by signs. In this system, the self is overwhelmed by the changes resulting from the convergence of markets, bureaucracies and electronic technologies. It is as though re-enchantment is occurring under a new form of charisma that cannot be centrally located in any individual or institution. Charisma as a pervasive power in the system of signs suggests an alternative approach to analysing religious experiences in the new millennium. This forms the task of the next chapter.

Notes

1 See Peter Gay (1977), *The Enlightenment*, 2 vols, New York: Norton.
2 Steven Seidman (1994), *Contested Knowledge*, Oxford: Blackwell, p.25.
3 Max Weber (1946), 'Science as a Vocation', in *From Max Weber: Essays in Sociology*, New York: Oxford University Press.
4 Ibid., p.152.
5 Anton C. Zijderveld (1970), *The Abstract Society*, London: Allen Lane, p.138.
6 Georg Lukács (1971), *History and Class Consciousness*, Cambridge, MA: MIT Press, p.83.
7 Ibid., p.104.
8 R. Hooykaas (1972), *Religion and the Rise of Modern Science*. Edinburgh: Scottish Academic Press, p.71.
9 Max Horkheimer and Theodor W. Adorno (1973), *Dialectic of Enlightenment*, London: Allen Lane (original 1947).
10 Ibid., p.9.
11 Ibid., p.24.
12 Ibid., p.121.
13 Ibid., pp.169–70.
14 Zygmunt Bauman (1989), *Modernity and the Holocaust*, Cambridge: Polity Press, p.70.
15 Jürgen Habermas (1984, 1987), *The Theory of Communicative Action*, 2 vols, Boston: Beacon.
16 Jürgen Habermas (1987), *The Philosophical Discourse of Modernity*, Cambridge, MA: MIT Press, p.304.
17 Finn Bowring (1996), 'A Lifeworld without a Subject: Habermas and the Pathologies of Modernity', *Telos*, (106), p.79.
18 There is a very large literature on secularization. See, for example, Thomas Luckmann (1967), *The Invisible Religion*, London: Macmillan; Richard K. Fenn (1978), *Toward a Theory of Secularization*, Storrs, CN: Society for the Scientific Study of Religion; David Martin (1978), *A General Theory of Secularization*, Oxford: Blackwell; Karel Dobbelaere (1981), 'Secularization: A Multi-Dimensional Concept', *Current Sociology*, 29, pp.1–216.
19 See, for example, Jeffrey K. Hadden (1987), 'Toward Desacralizing Secularization Theory', *Social Forces*, 65, pp.587–611; Steve Bruce (ed.) (1992), *Religion and Modernization*, Oxford: Clarendon Press.
20 This summary of semantic changes was derived from Michael Hill (1973), *A Sociology of Religion*, London: Heinemann, p.229.
21 See Karl Löwith (1949), *Meaning in History*, Chicago: University of Chicago Press; Hans Blumenberg (1983), *The Legitimation of the Modern Age*, Cambridge, MA: MIT Press.
22 Larry Shiner (1967), 'The Concept of Secularization in Empirical Research', *Journal for the Scientific Study of Religion*, 6, pp.202–20.
23 See, for example, Mark Chaves (1994), 'Secularization as Declining Religious Authority', *Social Forces*, 72, pp.749–74.
24 Bryan Wilson (1966), *Religion in Secular Society*, Harmondsworth: Penguin; Theodore Caplow (1985), 'Contrasting Trends in European and American Religion', *Sociological Analysis*, 46, pp.101–8.
25 Rodney Stark and William S. Bainbridge (1985), *The Future of Religion*, Berkeley, CA: University of California Press.
26 These tensions were first noted and discussed by Peter Berger (1969), *The Sacred Canopy*, New York: Anchor Books, p.108.
27 This paradox was also addressed by Bryan Wilson (1979), *Contemporary Transformations of Religion*, Oxford: Clarendon Press, p.99.

28 Anthony Giddens (1991), *Modernity and Self-Identity*, Cambridge: Polity Press, p.20.
29 For recent works on risk, see Ulrich Beck (1992), *Risk Society*, London: Sage; Niklas Luhmann (1993), *Risk: A Sociological Theory*, New York: Aldine de Gruyter; Mary Douglas (1994), *Risk and Blame*, London: Routledge.
30 David Martin (1978), *The Dilemmas of Contemporary Religion*, Oxford: Blackwell, p.69.
31 Ibid., p.70.
32 Ibid., p.92.
33 Alan D. Gilbert (1980), *The Making of Post-Christian Britain*, London: Longman, p.123.
34 Michael Löwy (1996), *The War of Gods: Religion and Politics in Latin America*, London: Verso, p.41.
35 David Martin (1990), *Tongues of Fire: The Explosion of Protestantism in Latin America*, Oxford: Blackwell.
36 Edward A. Tiryakian (1974), 'Toward the Sociology of Esoteric Culture', in E.A. Tiryakian (ed.), *On the Margin of the Visible: Sociology, the Esoteric, and the Occult*, New York: Wiley, pp.265–6.
37 See Paul Heelas (1996), *The New Age Movement*, Oxford: Blackwell.
38 Tiryakian, *On the Margin of the Visible*, *op. cit.*, p.274.
39 Ibid., pp.267–70.
40 See, for example, Anson D. Shupe and David G. Bromley (1980), *The New Vigilantes*, Beverly Hills: Sage; James A. Beckford (1985), *Cult Controversies*, London: Tavistock; Lewis Carter (1990), *Charisma and Control in Rajneeshpuram*, New York: Cambridge University Press.
41 These figures are from a survey of Western Buddhists in the mid-1990s conducted by Martin Baumann (1997),'The Dharma Has Come West: A Survey of Recent Studies and Sources', *Journal of Buddhist Ethics*, 4, pp.194–211.
42 Ibid., p.196.
43 Joseph B. Tamney (1992), *American Society in the Buddhist Mirror*, New York: Garland, pp.79, 157, 158.
44 Ibid., p.165.
45 Donald S. Lopez, Jr. (1998), *Prisoners of Shangri-La: Tibetan Buddhism and the West*, Chicago: University of Chicago Press, p.180. Independent institutions offering Buddhist studies programmes have also been set up in America, such as the Naropa Institute in Boulder, Colorado, the Namgyal Monastery Institute in Ithaca, New York, and Hsi Lai University in Rosemead, California. For other works that discuss the impact of Buddhism on the secular West, see Stephen Batchelor (1994), *The Awakening of the West: The Encounter of Buddhism and Western Culture*, Berkeley, CA: Parallax Press; Peter Bishop (1993), *Dreams of Power: Tibetan Buddhism and the Western Imagination*, Madison, NJ: Fairleigh Dickinson University Press.
46 For a historical meaning of the *Bardo Thödol* in English translation, see Lopez, *Prisoners of Shangri-La*, *op. cit.*, Chapter 2.
47 Both Tibetan and European Buddhist lamas qualified to teach *phowa* have offered their services to the public (for example, see advertisements appearing in the *Snow Lion Newsletter* between Fall 1995 and Fall 1998). A series of lectures on *phowa* given by a well-known Tibetan lama in 1981 has been published; see Lama Thubten Yeshe (1991), *Transference of Consciousness at the Time of Death*, Boston: Wisdom Publications.
48 James A. Beckford (1992), *Religion and Advanced Industrial Society*, London: Routledge, p.12.
49 See Roy Wallis (1984), *The Elementary Forms of the New Religious Life*, London: Routledge; Thomas Robbins (1988), 'Cults, Converts, and Charisma: The Sociology of New Religious Movements', *Current Sociology*, 36 (1), pp.1–256; William S. Bainbridge (1997), *The Sociology of Religious Movements*, London: Routledge.

50 Edward A. Tiryakian (1992), 'Dialectics of Modernity: Reenchantment and Dedifferentiation as Counterprocesses', in H. Haferkamp and N.J. Smelser (eds), *Social Change and Modernity*, Berkeley, CA: University of California Press, p.86.
51 Robert Wuthnow (1978), *Experimentation in American Religion*, Berkeley, CA: University of California Press, p.193.
52 George Ritzer (1995), *The McDonaldization of Society*, Thousand Oaks, CA: Sage.
53 Mark Gottdiener (1985), 'Hegemony and Mass Culture: A Socio-Semiotic Approach', *American Journal of Sociology*, 90, pp.979–1001.
54 This is the vision of writers such as Jean Baudrillard (1983), *Simulations*, New York: Semiotext(e) and idem (1993), *Symbolic Exchange and Death*. London: Sage.

Chapter 2

The Immanence of Charisma

Charisma is probably one of the most misunderstood words in the analysis of religious actions and movements. It is a word fraught with mystery and power, usually assigned to describe or explain the magnetic personality of a leader or the extraordinary means by which social and religious change is accomplished. The word has remained firmly embedded in the sociology of religion for identifying a residual category of unconventional behaviour or transformative force.

One reason for this residual status is the difficulty with which radical change is accommodated in the Western Enlightenment paradigm. This paradigm, as discussed in Chapter 1, concerns social developments that are said to be linear and progressive. The Hegelian notion of dialectical change is not alien to this paradigm because it posits the juxtaposition of opposing forces as natural to the evolution of society. On the one hand, charisma implies a supernatural force that can interrupt or reverse the natural progression of societal development. Thus, charisma suggests the recognition of a powerful but disruptive force that threatens the process of rationalization in society. Charisma constitutes a wild card in the Enlightenment paradigm.

A post-Enlightenment paradigm suggests that charisma be treated not simply as a revolutionary force or an exceptional trait of leadership, but as a specific outcome of immanent power in the world. By this definition, religious innovation would not be considered as necessarily threatening a social order. The implicit reference to charisma as something irrational is thereby abandoned.

Charisma, as an expression of this immanent power, provides the vehicle for the transformation of identities without necessarily implying the formation of new social structures. This is not the same as saying that there is no real social change, but that change can occur without the possibility of structural innovation followed by routinization. It is in routinization that the apparent irrationality of charisma is brought under control. However, charismatic action without routinization suggests that the cultivation of immanent power cannot be effectively rationalized into a body of disenchantment.

The task of this chapter is to reconceptualize charisma as an immanent power linked to re-enchantment. This approach suggests that the process of routinization is not necessarily an inevitable outcome of charismatic action. Before we get to this point, we will discuss the conventional meaning of charisma as a problem of social control.

The Taming of Charisma

What makes charisma such a beguiling concept is its seemingly unrestrained expression of power outside the boundaries of tradition and bureaucracy. This is the distinction between the power of extraordinary means and established structures of control in Max Weber's classical comparison of the different forms of authority.[1] He wanted to show that structural authority in tradition and bureaucracy was always confronted by a powerful, irrational force of change. In a way, Weber was intrigued by the nature of authority originating in the awe-inspiring actions of a virtuoso who formed a special bond with his followers. This type of authority was special in the sense that it transcended the boundaries of what was normally called traditional or bureaucratic. However, the unbridled power of charisma seemed to have instilled a sense of apprehension in Weber who probably saw the necessity of transforming the irrationality of this power into a conventional authority through the process of routinization.[2]

Although Weber popularized the sociological use of the term 'charisma', he was not the first person to bring its social meaning to scholarly attention.[3] It was the German legal scholar, Rudolph Sohm, who initially applied the term to his studies on the organization of the early Christian community.[4] For Sohm, charisma was an important concept for understanding the dynamics of the early apostolic Christian community and its eventual transformation into the vast Roman Catholic Church. He had no intention of sociologizing the term as a peculiar attribute of individual leaders and its impact on religious organizations and movements. Rather, charisma was treated as 'moral commands which decided questions about the ethical life of the individual as well as, directly or indirectly, questions about the life and division of the ecclesia'.[5] Sohm's reference to charisma was specifically collective in the sense of a moral culture that differed from other cultures. The unity of this culture was based on, and reflected, a charismatic power that could not be identified with any individual.

Sohm argued that the charisma of the early Christian community did not survive because it was obliterated by a process that he termed 'legalization'. The end result of this process was the impersonal structure of the Roman Catholic Church. This process occurred through three stages, beginning with the letter of Clement sent to the Christians in Corinth around 100 CE that signalled the establishment of a monarchical episcopate. Following this, the circulation of the letter of Ignatius in 115 CE provided a decree for the subordination of all independent assemblies to the bishop's assembly. Finally, legalization was completed by the bishop's assumption of office that empowered him to decide what constituted right opinion.[6]

It was Sohm's idea of the legalization process in the early Christian community that led Weber to propose the routinization of charisma. Routinization referred to the process by which the awe-inspiring power of a charismatic leader was attenuated and regulated by the development of an institution built on that power. Weber identified three stages of routinization in which individual leaders 'wish to see their positions transformed from purely factual power relations into a cosmos of acquired rights, and to know that they are thus sanctified'.[7] These stages involved leadership succession through: 'the sacramental substantiation of charisma' or 'a belief in hereditary charisma'; the establishment of rules that became the basis of tradition; and the transformation of disciples and followers into bureaucrats and officials.[8]

In Weber's thinking, it was not the moral teachings that became routinized but the personal authority of the charismatic leader once he transferred his powers to the systematic command of office. Weberian scholars who assumed this line of argument were in effect asserting the abnegation of charisma through the process of institutionalization. The power of the institution seemed to overwhelm and absorb the original charismatic source of inspiration and social action.[9]

Weber's adoption and modification of Sohm's idea have become the cornerstone for contemporary sociological research on charisma.[10] The focus of this research is on the individualistic meaning of charisma for the analysis of social and religious change. As a result, charisma exemplifies an anti-modern or revolutionary tendency that defies bureaucratic power or any form of traditional authority. It is a movement of de-institutionalization that questions, challenges and threatens the power elite in religion and politics. This type of movement is charismatic because one of its characteristics is the creation of strong emotional bonds between the leader and his followers. Intense feelings of awe, loyalty and devotion are expressed by followers in exchange for the charismatic leader's alleged ability to grant them victory in all endeavours and to lead them to a better world. These emotional ties imply that, very often, bonding between a charismatic leader and his followers lacks a rational or intellectual basis. The followers are dependent on the will and behaviour of the charismatic leader for the fulfilment of their wants and needs, not because of some well-thought-out arrangements but because of their emotional investment in his leadership.

The personal nature of charisma implies an individualized form of power. The special abilities of a charismatic leader are not shared by, or distributed among, members close to him. What happens to this power when the leader dies? In cases where a successor has been chosen, charisma is passed down, so to speak, from the leader to disciple or next of kin. Charismatic power does not end with the leader's passing, but is inherited by those who come after him. If disputes arise over the question of succession, charisma may become splintered in the sense that contenders for leadership 'make off' with some of the original charisma by establishing separate followings and movements. Hence, charisma loses its exclusiveness in struggles of succession.

As the inheritors of charisma settle into offices of administration, a particular hierarchy or structure of authority is formed and gradually takes on an appearance of independent power. Even after the charismatic successors have passed on, this appearance of independent power does not fade away but lives on as 'institutionalized charisma'. This simply means that people may just feel overwhelmed by the tremendous power concentrated in some structures of authority such as those found in political and military organizations. It is at this juncture that we see how the meaning of routinization comes to suggest the loss in these organizations of the personal and innovative dimension witnessed in the original charismatic expression of the leader. Charisma is no longer considered a threat because it is trapped and subdued by the fate of its own development into a labyrinthine structure.

There is another type of charisma that has emerged in modernity but has little to do with de-institutionalization. It is a type that is nurtured by modern institutions. Glassman called this type 'manufactured charisma' because it is a product of institutional activities, an invention of the mass media, or an image presentation of advertising wizards.[11] To understand the meaning of manufactured charisma, Glassman sought to compare it with charisma found in late tribal and early agricultural societies. In those societies, which were characterized by intense succession struggles, the charismatic process was stage-managed to keep power within clans. But this type of charisma was not immune to challenges from natural charismatic leadership, which stemmed from the revolutionary powers of a single person. In modernity, however, the high-tech facilities of the mass media enable more sensational and spectacular displays of charisma, which could keep audiences in awe indefinitely and maintain the legitimacy of those in power. Manufactured charisma lives on modern technology, and appears dazzling and innovative for the purpose of renewing people's faith in existing institutions. Generally, it has no revolutionary qualities.

The common theme in all these accounts of charisma concerns the institutional control of the spontaneous exuberance of personal power. It reflects an underlying apprehension of the primeval wellspring of inspirational power. Sohm's 'legalization', Weber's 'routinization' and Glassman's 'manufactured charisma' could be said to represent a means of confronting this fear by subordinating this power to the crushing weight of modern institutions. Yet, the source of this power is not easily diminished.

An Alternative to Routinization

The Enlightenment paradigm provided the canvas on which charisma was painted into a corner. Charisma was 'legalized' or 'routinized' into a rationally staid pattern of bureaucratic control replete with rank of office and hierarchical positions. In a sense, the Enlightenment paradigm accentuated the transparency of institutional power through a disclosure of its charismatic origins, but stopped short of sanctifying those origins as the antediluvian basis of religious authority and group formation. Instead, the paradigmatic assumption of linear progression turned charismatic origins into a victim of historical movement to be engulfed and overcome by the processes of institution-building. Within this paradigm, charisma led a doomed existence.

The Enlightenment paradigm provides the rational parameters for anticipating secularization. It means that secularization as an unfolding process of desacralization marginalizes the charismatic origins of religious authority. This is accomplished by transforming charisma into a form of institutional control. In short, secularization contains the blueprint for routinizing charisma. But secularization itself is a remarkably complex phenomenon that opens up individual choices, cultural preferences and social innovations. By desacralizing religious authority, secularization ironically frees the individual from traditional religious obligations only to invigorate the individual's search for existential meaning in the realm of the extraordinary. In this circular process, charisma is diminished by routinization, but revived in different ways through an impulse for re-enchantment implicit in the secularization process itself.

At the centre of this circular process is the individual self, which is both the source of charismatic expression and the locus of routinization. Through the self, charisma is embodied as a special manifestation of divine power. But secularization causes contradictions in the self, distancing it from the sacred derivatives of charisma by regular exposure to the routines of office. On the other hand, the multiple realities made available to the self in secularized existence tend to problematize the meaning of that existence. Transcendence of that existence is likely to regenerate the self's quest for charismatic inspiration. Thus, the idea of routinization and its paradoxical effect on meaning cannot be simply addressed as a problem of structural transformation. The self is vital to the charismatic imagination.

The strong presence of the self in charisma may be attributed to Weber's long-standing struggle to locate agency in social change. Charisma represents the desideratum in the self's sudden descent into irrationality as a special condition for explaining the power of agency in altering history. The routinization of this self-centred charisma is, in effect, a statement on the need to restore equanimity to the wild fluctuations of an empowered self in the process of activating change. As long as the self predominates in the processes of social change, the concept of routinization would be seen as a necessary device for restoring the sense of order to the turbulence of change experienced by the self. But if the self is not featured as central to the processes of social change, charisma takes on a different shade of meaning and routinization becomes a superfluous idea.

An alternative to routinization entails the decentring of charisma in order to remove the presence of the self as an agent of change.[12] Instead, charisma is conceptualized as an immanent power without explicit association to individual consciousness, behaviour and action. In this respect, charisma represents a unique source of empowerment not embodied in human agents, but transmitted through ritual action, interpretation and belief. The immanence of charisma simply means that it is not a property of individuals, although specific individuals can claim to manifest it. From this position, it can be argued that a 'self-less' charisma cannot be routinized.

There are two ways of presenting the above argument. First, the immanence of charisma suggests that there is nothing particularly mysterious or awesome about it, unless it is thought of as such in power-related situations. The special quality of charisma is largely a function of the social definitions given to the manifestations claimed by a leader and seemingly demonstrated to his followers. Routinization does not apply to charisma but to the power relations between leaders, disciples and the population at large. In other words, there is a kind of versatility in charisma that enables it to fulfil the special relationship between leaders and followers. It is the fulfilment of this relationship that eventually becomes routinized, but not the impersonal power underlying that fulfilment.

Second, the pervasiveness of charisma allows it to reorder the meaning of existence in multiple ways that defy conventional form. This means that it is not charisma that is endemic to change, but change that is endemic to charisma. It is as though contact with charisma necessitates transformation. It cannot be routinized because its transformative power opposes all conventionalities. As a power of renewal, charisma overcomes all forms of regularity, hierarchy and uniformity. The establishment of any order following significant events of transformation implies that charisma can no longer be identified as irrevocably present – it has moved on, so to speak. Such an approach to charisma has important implications for understanding the contemporary meaning of re-enchantment. But, first, it is necessary to demonstrate how these ideas can be applied to actual circumstances.

The Power of the Word

The immanence of charisma allows it to be encoded into a specific form to structure social definitions and relations of power. These codes are constituted by cultural and linguistic meanings that ostensibly reduce charisma into a set of relationships. Scriptural texts and other symbolic representations of sacredness are examples of the way in which charisma becomes encoded into concrete reality. They are the encoded transformations of a 'self-less' charisma into an object of power.

When the object of power is treated only as a symbol and its referent assigned to a separate source, the encoding of charisma may be termed dualistic in the sense that the symbol stands for a greater power, which is hidden and removed from the human realm. This hidden power is seen as the primeval referent of charisma and individuals approach it through the symbolic object represented in linguistic code as a scriptural text. The text itself is not necessarily regarded as divinity but as a bridge, enriched by cultural interpretations, to the experience of divinity.

In Islam, the Qur'an represents the revealed word of God transmitted to the prophet Muhammad by the archangel Gabriel. According to Denny, 'the Qur'an as complete book is simply a collection of a great number of separate recitations revealed to Muhammad over the entire course of his prophetic career, first in Mecca and later in Medina'.[13] Collection of all these recitations was said to have begun during Muhammad's lifetime, but the task was not completed until the reign of the Third Caliph, Uthman, in the mid-seventh century. These were not mere recitations, but divine revelations (*wahyu*) transmitted to Muhammad whose alleged illiteracy has been taken as proof of his 'inability to have composed the Qur'an himself and thus safeguards its divine provenance and inimitability'.[14]

The power of the Qur'an, therefore, reflects the original charisma experienced by Muhammad on the night the archangel Gabriel first appeared to him and over the years of visionary contact. During his lifetime, Muhammad could indeed be said to have 'possessed' charisma because of the growing belief in the authenticity of his mission and his success in winning converts. Even his own utterances, which were eventually recorded and preserved as *hadith*, came to wield considerable influence, thus suggesting that his charisma was not confined to his revelatory experiences. But, with his passing in 632 CE, the meaning of charisma could no longer be considered a personal manifestation of divine power – although this power remained. It is in the notion of a decentred charisma that this power could be seen as encoded in a holy scripture.

Thus, the Qur'an in its original Arabic rendition symbolizes not the exemplary behaviour or special status of the prophet Muhammad (who allegedly refused to take credit for the Qur'an[15]), but a divine message imbued with charisma that is immanent in the Muslim universe of believers. As Denny put it, "The Qur'an teaches the faithful what to believe, and in the process assures them of the efficacy of their faithfulness by means of its mysterious powers'.[16] These mysterious powers emanate from the charismatic referent, which is not the same as the Qur'an but is symbolized by it, and the belief of all Muslims in the efficacy of the holy book.

What have been routinized over the course of Islamic history are not those mysterious powers but the cultural meanings and practices attributed to Qur'anic discourses. These meanings and practices are found in the Islamic institutions of *kuttab* (that teaches proper recitation of the Qur'an) and *tafsir* (the traditional and allegorical exegesis of the Qur'an). The original charisma that changed Muhammad's life and inspired his mission and the recording of the divine message remains at large.

Like the Qur'an, the Hindu Vedas are regarded as revealed scriptures (*sruti*). These revelations were experienced by Vedic seers (*rishi*) more than three millennia ago and transmitted by their disciples who, in turn, passed them on to their disciples. Their transcription into Sanskrit scriptures came later, but cannot be traced to any specific author. Lester pointed out that, despite the unbroken chain of transmission in the Vedas, no indication of human origin could be discerned.[17] This lack of human origin suggests that the charismatic source of the revelations remains relatively undisturbed in the sense of minimal human mediation and distortion. The correct chanting of the Vedas has been preserved for generations, since deviations are believed to render ritual actions ineffective. The Vedas, therefore, represent a reservoir of charisma first experienced by Indian *rishis* and, through the mantra-form, the Vedic word connects the worshipper with the decentred power of the universe.[18]

Unlike the Qur'an, the Vedas are not associated with a prophet or an emissary of God. This implies that the personal element of charismatic inspiration is highly reduced in Vedic religion. The *rishis* who originally experienced the revelations may have 'possessed' charisma, but the absence of their identities attenuates its subjective dimension. Hence, the power of the word predominates in Vedic rites and practices. Invoked in the proper manner, the Vedic word enables the flow of charisma.

As with the example of the Qur'anic word, the concept of routinization cannot be directly applied to the Vedic word because its representation of the original revelations remains pristine through an unbroken chain of transmission. However, the secondary works emerging from the Vedic word (known collectively as the Vedanga) may be considered as having been subjected to the routines of discourse and practice over the centuries. These works cover etymology, grammar, phonetics, astrology, ritual performance and exegesis.[19] Together, they comprise the institutionalized forms of Sanskrit speech, morals and philosophy that is referred to as *smriti* (that which is remembered). It is in *smriti* that routinization is observed, since it is the area in which human relationships are regulated with regard to speech and behaviour.

These two examples of the Qur'an and the Vedas set the word-as-symbol apart from the charisma of the original revelations. But, in other religious practices, the symbol itself is regarded as the power. In this case, the non-distinction between the symbol and referent may be termed 'sign-power'. Charisma in sign-power is decentred in the sense that it is not attributed to a particular word, person or event, but is readily experienced through the proper merging of the mind with a symbol. Here, the symbol is both the vehicle and power of mind concentration that results in charismatic experience. An example is the Hindu and Buddhist notion of *mandala*.

The *mandala* is different from the word because it is not represented in the form of alphabets or sounds, but as diagrams designed symmetrically with circles, squares and triangles. These diagrams are also filled with representations of deities. There are several literal meanings of *mandala*. Eliade referred to it as circle or surroundings,[20] whereas Trungpa defined it as association or society.[21] Metaphorically, a *mandala* denotes a pattern of power for transcending ordinary reality. It is a diagrammatic instrument for realizing the charisma of primordial unity.

The *mandala* is an important object of mental support in meditation and ritual action.[22] As in the initiation ceremony of the *mandala* described by Eliade, the person who is initiated is given instructions, among other things, to merge with the *mandala*. In Eliade's words, 'as soon as he entered the *mandala*, he is in a sacred space, outside of time.... In a vision, he sees [the gods] emerge and spring from his heart; they fill cosmic space, then are reabsorbed in him.'[23] Thus, the *mandala* experience is essentially a holistic experience that empowers the individual through a profound sense of oneness. Trungpa also emphasized this experience of totality: 'The total mandala, the mandala of totality, is not dependent on boundaries at all. Therefore, its expressions are regarded as different aspects of one totality.'[24]

The examples of the Qur'an, the Vedas and the *mandala* convey the sense of charisma as an impersonal power, hidden from view but accessed through ritual actions based on the symbolic codes of the holy scriptures or the *mandala*. This power is not dependent on the agency of a particular individual, but is immanent in the belief system of the practitioners. It cannot be routinized except in the ritual and discursive legacies of religious institutions. In other words, there is a sense of transparency in this power that allows for the diversity of expression without the centrality of location. The immanence of this power implies that it cannot be treated as a particular substance with specific features. The shape of this power depends on the social and cultural circumstances that make possible its expression. Hence, it is the expression of this power (but not the power itself) that is susceptible to institutionalization.

Charisma in the New Age

The immanence of charisma suggests that the route to re-enchantment cannot be completely displaced by the forces of modernity because rationalization is merely a veneer of institutional control that cannot effectively subdue a power without a centre. Particularly in the New Age, the belief that the self is essentially a free agent traversing a diverse field of alternative religions reinforces the idea of immanent charisma. Analysed by many researchers, the New Age refers to an eclectic range of unconventional religious movements and practices that are traceable to the occult tradition, neo-paganism and the counterculture in the West.[25] Most participants in New Age movements believe in spiritual evolution through self-transformation. The cosmocentrism and monistic tendencies in these movements suggest that self-transformation in the New Age is empowered by charisma, which is not centrally located but pervasive in magical and holistic actions.

The New Age exemplifies the trend towards re-enchantment at the beginning of the twenty-first century. It brings together the themes of healing, self-determinism and transcendental consciousness in a variety of movements that challenge the ethos of disenchantment, and reintroduce the idea of the magical as something that binds empirical and spiritual realities in a continuous relationship. Catherine Albanese considers this form of re-enchantment as a return to nature religion. She identified healing as central to a consciousness that reunites the empirical and spiritual dimensions of the human experience.[26] It is the healing aspect of nature religion that activates an immanent charisma conjoining the empirical and spiritual. Re-enchantment is, therefore, another way of opening up the self to an immanent charisma that does not differentiate between the inner and outer realms of human existence. This was what Heelas meant when he described New Age healing as coming from within one's self or 'from one's *own* experience of the natural order as a whole'.[27]

Immanent charisma is a motif of New Age healing, but it is also subjected to the spiritual logic of late capitalism. As suggested in the previous chapter, the New Age is a product of the late capitalist era where secularization has spawned an emporium of salvationary choices. In the New Age, individual seekers have greater freedom than their predecessors to explore and participate in a wide variety of alternative religions. At the same time, New Age religious experimentation occurs in a context of volatile markets and rapidly changing consumer trends. There is nothing more divinely materialistic than the New Age emphasis on 'a harmonious union of spirituality and prosperity, religious transcendence and success in capitalist business'.[28] Hence, New Age seekers develop no sense of guilt or inhibition in integrating the quest for spiritual liberation and materialistic indulgence.

The emergence of New Age tantrism illustrates the conjunction of religious fervour and late capitalist morality. Tantrism has roots in the Hindu religious system, particularly as a branch of esoteric practice that was considered antinomian and mystically powerful. Although rarely described as charismatic, tantrism as both a discourse and practice of inner energies can be said to exemplify an arcane method for the manipulation of immanent charisma. In other words, tantrism personifies the unseen or pervasive power of nature. Its attraction in the New Age is consistent with the re-enchantment of nature. But the burgeoning of New Age tantrism is, according to Hugh Urban's analysis, 'the ideal expression of and religion for late twentieth-century consumer capitalist society'.[29] He argues that New Age tantrism, as a path to spiritual liberation, not only rejects established Western ideologies but also celebrates 'an aesthetic of intensity, hedonism, and shock'.[30] In the context of freewheeling consumerism, online ecstasies and market mechanisms, New Age tantrism is likely to yield responses that possess sign, rather than symbolic, value.

The sign, discussed in the preceding chapter, refers to a form of representation without reference to other objects. Signs behave as though they are their own realities. In the case of New Age tantrism, the messages and methods of spiritual liberation have been disconnected from their traditional sources to constitute self-defining icons of religious experimentation. Thus, in his survey of tantric websites on the Internet, Urban describes this emerging network as if seekers were navigating through a territory of signs. He says, 'The net surfer can now enter a number of Tantric temples and mandalas and experience virtual *darshan* of a host of Tantric deities, all at a click of a mouse and via a high-speed modem and the appropriate software.'[31]

As tantrism is reduced to mouse-clicks, virtual temples and online rituals, the meaning of charisma as an immanent force becomes even more relevant. By accessing tantrism on the Internet, a seeker is virtually experiencing the transformative power of nature through the pervasiveness of cyberspace. Even though tantrism is symbolically connected to particular virtuosos and texts, its presence on the Internet suggests an autonomous field of esotericism signified by digital power. In a sense, tantric charisma on the Internet resembles Glassman's 'manufactured charisma', since it is dependent on modern technology for its dissemination. But unlike the institutional bases of 'manufactured charisma', the charisma of New Age tantrism is not defined by fixed hierarchies and authority structures. New Age seekers are free to come and go from tantric websites without experiencing any sense of pressure or commitment to become fully-fledged tantric practitioners.

The charisma of New Age tantrism, therefore, cannot be routinized in the Weberian sense of the word. Since tantric teachings and methods are now widely available on the Internet, the charisma associated with tantrism cannot be reined in by the structures of authority. Every seeker can now virtually click on to several tantric websites and experience tantric charisma without submitting to the authority of any guru. In the digital culture of late capitalism, the consumer mentality provides a limiting condition to routinization because charisma can be transformed into a commodity for personal experience without institutional requirements.

The cultural syncretism of the New Age has not only refurbished tantrism with the sign values of the Internet, but also opened up new ways of charismatic expression. The appearance of reincarnated lamas in Western Buddhism exemplifies the myriad possibilities of charismatic transformation in the New Age. The belief in reincarnation is fundamental to Buddhism, but in the Tibetan Buddhist system, reincarnated lamas are perceived as a source and expression of charismatic power.[32] A reincarnated lama is referred to as a *tulku*. He is recognized as having inherited charisma from his predecessor who is none other than himself in another identity from another lifetime.

According to Michael, since the twelfth century all the major sects in Tibetan Buddhism have recognized the institution of lama reincarnation.[33] This is an institution that has ostensibly preserved and routinized charisma in a religious hierarchy or hierocracy. Yet it is not sufficient to describe this institution as merely an instance of the routinization of charisma. The Tibetan hierocracy may be described as a particular manifestation of power relations based on an ancient shamanic tradition. It is this tradition that is charismatic, and this charisma may be interpreted as the efficacy of collective belief in the magical performances of a tradition rooted in the pre-Buddhist Bön religion of Tibet. Eliade has remarked that '[e]ven the most famous masters of Tibetan Buddhism are reputed to have performed cures and worked miracles in the purest tradition of shamanism'.[34] Thus, there is only an appearance of routinization, but in reality charismatic power in shamanic form continues to influence important activities within the hierocracy.

It can be seen from this brief allusion to the shamanic aspects of the Tibetan hierocracy that charisma in the Tibetan religious system is far from routinized. Charisma is considered indispensable to the enactment of rituals and healing by members of the Tibetan hierocracy. Belief in the reality of reincarnated lamas provides the faith for reproducing the manifestation of such charisma. Thus, it is not the *tulku* who personally becomes the centre of charismatic expression, but his position as an official site for the manifestation of immanent charisma. In this sense, we can describe the *tulku* as the bearer of charismatic structure.

Throughout Tibetan religious history, the reproduction of charisma through the *tulku* system has not extended beyond the central Asian region. All this changed in 1985. The birth of Osel Hita Torres in Granada, Spain that year signalled a new beginning in the ethnic identity of *tulkus*. The parents of Osel were devout followers of Lama Thubten Yeshe, a well-known Tibetan lama who had introduced Buddhism to many Europeans and Americans. Lama Yeshe passed away in 1984 and was cremated in California. His disciple, Lama Zopa, spent the following months searching for the rebirth of his guru. Guided by his dreams, Lama Zopa finally identified Osel as the reincarnation of Lama Yeshe.[35]

The fact that the Dalai Lama (the spiritual and temporal head of the Tibetan community) has officially recognized Osel as the reincarnation of Lama Yeshe enhances the image of the Tibetan hierocracy as being open to change. This change occurred at a time when Tibetan Buddhism became popular in the West. Since the identification of this Spanish boy as a *tulku*, there have been other reports of lama reincarnations in the West. At least three other Western *tulkus* have been tracked down and written up by Mackenzie.[36]

The phenomenon of the Western *tulkus* illustrates the transformative capacity of charisma. As argued earlier, charisma as a power of renewal overcomes tradition and conventionality. The appearance of Western *tulkus* without strong opposition from the Tibetan hierocracy and community suggests an acceptance of change that is consonant with the transformative potential implied in the charisma of reincarnation. It is as though the charisma of reincarnation points the way to new relations between the Tibetan hierocracy and Western devotees through a redefinition of *tulku* identity.

For many devotees of Tibetan Buddhism, the *tulku* system represents an unbroken chain of charisma within the Tibetan community. But in the context of the New Age, this chain has been altered to include Westerners. This change suggests that the *tulku* system only maintains an appearance of routinization, but the flexibility of the system in introducing innovations undermines that appearance. The different careers of the Western *tulkus*, as described by Mackenzie, give the impression that charisma cannot be unilaterally routinized because the transference of the *tulku* system to the West has opened up more alternatives and choices than had been traditionally available in Tibet. Western *tulkus* may undergo spiritual training in Tibetan monasteries as part of a traditional routine, but that training does not necessarily determine the direction of their careers in a routinized sense. They are free to decide on taking the vows of monkhood or to choose other careers that may or may not be spiritual in nature.

These two examples of New Age tantrism and Western *tulkus* demonstrate the immanence of charisma in the processes of re-enchantment. Particularly in the context of late capitalism, the charisma of tantrism and reincarnation is manifested through a sign system that abrogates references to tradition. Tantric websites and Western *tulkus* are not traditional, so to speak, because they are innovations of the New Age. Hence, logging on to a tantric website does not require prior knowledge of the tantric tradition. The phenomenon of the Western *tulku* is unprecedented in the Tibetan Buddhist tradition.

Thus, New Age religious innovations exist as signs in a market-like situation that thrives on syncretic ideas and practices. Charisma associated with signs has an eclectic quality not bound to any hierarchy or institution. It differs from the charisma of the holy word discussed earlier. The latter constitutes a power initially experienced by prophets and seers, and later encoded as a text. As symbol, the holy word stands for sources of tradition embedded in divine revelations. The symbolism of the holy word is maintained not by market processes, but by an unfaltering belief in the charisma of textual representation. When this belief is renewed in the context of acute social conflict, it crystallizes into the phenomenon of fundamentalism. Fundamentalism is, therefore, not merely a defence of religious tradition, but a celebration of textual charisma (see Chapter 4). Whether charisma is manifested under the symbol or sign depends on the 'regime of signification' experienced by the middle classes whose role in the processes of re-enchantment cannot be overlooked. The next chapter concerns the meaning of re-enchantment in the middle classes.

Notes

1 See Max Weber (1946), *From Max Weber: Essays in Sociology*, New York: Oxford University Press; and idem (1968), *Economy and Society*, New York: Bedminster Press.

2 Weber's uneasiness with the irrational has been noted and discussed in various works. See H. Stuart Hughes (1961), *Consciousness and Society*, New York: Vintage, pp.303–4;

Donald Levine (1981), 'Rationality and Freedom: Weber and Beyond', *Sociological Inquiry*, 51, pp.5–25; Jukka Gronow (1988), 'The Element of Irrationality: Max Weber's Diagnosis of Modern Culture', *Acta Sociologica* , 31, pp.319–31; Alan Sica (1988), *Weber, Irrationality, and Social Order*, Berkeley, CA: University of California Press.

3 This was noted by Julian Freund (1969), *The Sociology of Max Weber*, London: Penguin, p.232.

4 The contributions of Sohm and the implications of his work for the sociological meaning of charisma have been closely examined in an unpublished dissertation by Peter D. Haley (1980), 'The Idea of Charismatic Authority: From Theology to Sociology', unpublished PhD dissertation, University of Pennsylvania. Our discussion of Sohm's work is based largely on Haley's dissertation.

5 Ibid., p.31.

6 Ibid., pp.66–76. It is interesting to note that recent sociological analysis of early Christianity no longer depends on the notion of charisma. In Rodney Stark's *The Rise of Christianity*, San Francisco: HarperCollins, 1997, the author dismissed charisma as 'only a name that too often is thought to explain something, but does not' (p.24). Instead, he explained the strength of the early Christian community in behavioural terms such as high commitment, resource mobilization, and credible religious compensators. By jettisoning charisma, Stark did not have to deal with the problem of irrationality. He could focus his analysis on the rational aspects of religious organization and growth (p.167ff).

7 Weber, *From Max Weber, op.cit.*, p.262.

8 Ibid., p.297.

9 See for instance, Edward Shils (1965), 'Charisma, Order, and Status', *American Sociological Review*, 30, pp.199–213.

10 For example, see R.S. Perinbayanagam (1971),'The Dialectics of Charisma', *The Sociological Quarterly*, 12, pp.387–402; Charles P. Cell (1974), 'Charismatic Heads of State: The Social Context', *Behavioral Science Research*, 9, pp.255–305; Martin E. Spencer (1973), 'What is Charisma?' *British Journal of Sociology*, 24, pp.341–54; Charles Camic (1980), 'Charisma: Its Varieties, Preconditions, and Consequences', *Sociological Inquiry*, 50, pp.5–23; William H. Swatos, Jr. (1981), 'The Disenchantment of Charisma: A Weberian Assessment of Revolution in a Rationalized World', *Sociological Analysis*, 42, pp.119–36.

11 Ronald Glassman (1975), 'Legitimacy and Manufactured Charisma', *Social Research*, 42, pp.615–36.

12 The idea of decentring can be traced to French poststructuralism. This theoretical perspective de-emphasizes the self as the vantage point from which everything is evaluated. Rather, it takes language as a structure of relational positions that produces meaning. Thus a decentred world operates on impersonal forces from which the illusion of interacting selves is fabricated. For a general understanding of this perspective, see Madan Sarup (1993), *An Introductory Guide to Post-Structuralism and Postmodernism*, Athens, GA: University of Georgia Press.

13 Frederick M. Denny (1985), 'Islam: Qur'an and Hadith', in F.M. Denny and R.L. Taylor (eds), *The Holy Book in Comparative Perspective*, Columbia, SC: University of South Carolina Press, pp.86–7.

14 Ibid., p.85.

15 Ibid., p.88.

16 Ibid., p.103.

17 Robert C. Lester (1985), 'Hinduism: Veda and Sacred Texts', in F.M. Denny and R.L. Taylor (eds.), *The Holy Book*, p.138.

18 The mantra form in Hinduism invokes power by the precise recitation of specific Sanskrit words arranged in short lines or stanzas. Even a special word or two can be treated as a mantra. The rhythm, tone and frequency of recitation constitute the method of activating a mantra.

19 See Lester, 'Hinduism', *op.cit.*, pp.133–9.
20 Mircea Eliade (1969), *Yoga: Immortality and Freedom*, Princeton, NJ: Princeton University Press, p.219.
21 Chögyam Trungpa (1991), *Orderly Chaos: The Mandala Principle*, Boston, MA: Shambala, p.15.
22 See Giuseppe Tucci (1961), *The Theory and Practice of the Mandala*, London: Rider.
23 Eliade, Yoga, *op.cit.*, p.225.
24 Trungpa, *Orderly Chaos*, *op.cit.*, p.90.
25 See Gordon Melton (1990), *New Age Encyclopedia*, Detroit, MI: Gale Research; James Lewis and Gordon Melton (eds.) (1992), *Perspectives on the New Age*, Albany, NY: State University of New York Press; Michael York (1995), *The Emerging Network: A Sociology of New Age and New Religious Movements*, Lanham, MD: Rowman and Littlefield; Paul Heelas (1996), *The New Age Movement*, Oxford: Blackwell.
26 Catherine L. Albanese (1993), 'Fisher Kings and Public Places: The Old New Age in the 1990s', *Annals of the American Academy of Political and Social Science*, 527, 131-143.
27 Heelas, *op. cit.*, p.82.
28 Hugh B. Urban (2000), 'The Cult of Ecstasy: Tantrism, the New Age, and the Spiritual Logic of Late Capitalism', *History of Religions*, 39, pp.268–304 at p.277.
29 Ibid., p.295.
30 Ibid., p.299.
31 Ibid., p.293.
32 The Tibetan lama is a Buddhist monk or preceptor generally respected for his high learning, spiritual knowledge, and practice of compassion. Disciples and laymen perceive the lama as the fount of the Tibetan Buddhist system. See Geoffrey Samuel (1995), *Civilized Shamans: Buddhism in Tibetan Societies*, Washington DC: Smithsonian Institution.
33 Franz Michael (1982), *Rule by Incarnation: Tibetan Buddhism and Its Role in Society and State*, Boulder, CO: Westview Press, p.2.
34 Mircea Eliade (1964), *Shamanism: Archaic Techniques of Ecstasy*, Princeton, NJ: Princeton University Press, p.434.
35 An account of this event can be found in Vicki Mackenzie (1988), *Reincarnation: The Boy Lama*, London: Bloomsbury.
36 Vicki Mackenzie (1996), *Reborn in the West: The Reincarnation Masters*, New York: Marlowe & Company. Even Hollywood action star, Steven Seagal, has been identified as a *tulku* (see 'Tinseltown Tulku', in *Tricycle: The Buddhist Review*, 6(4), Summer 1997, p.81.

Chapter 3

The Re-enchantment of the Middle Classes

Middle-class society as a global phenomenon is the site of religious developments that appear to be reversing disenchantment. However, intensified religious consciousness in the middle classes is occurring under the peculiar conditions of late capitalism that have redefined middle-class identity and the search for transcendental meanings. As capital becomes more diverse and globalized, multiple forms of consciousness and activity develop in the middle classes. Re-enchantment of the middle classes is not only a reaction to the world of technological control and bureaucratic routines, but also a consequence of an emerging regime of signification dominated by the sign. To understand how re-enchantment is occurring in the middle classes, we will first elucidate the conditions of late capitalism.

The Effects of Late Capitalism

The character of middle-class society has become more complex as capital concentrates into larger units and expands on a global scale. A bewildering diversity of intermediate strata is produced in response to the high degree of specialization required by global capital. Middle-class social locations and forms of consciousness are now found in a division of labour delegated to, and dispersed over, proliferating intermediate strata.[1] Reproduction of the labour force, control and conceptualization are carried out by increasingly specialized groups making up the diffuse middle classes. This class structure rests upon an extensive bureaucratic organization that sustains both disenchantment and reification.

Middle-class specialists employed in large organizations experience their work conditions as predictable and standardized. But they also experience a sense of individual autonomy that allows the novel production of cultural forms. In other words, the activity of the middle classes produces an abstract and highly specialized socioeconomic system pervaded by limitless cultural meanings. These contradictory directions of middle-class activity break down the experience of social totality into segmented and disconnected worlds. Consequently, ambiguity becomes a perpetual condition of the middle classes.

The juxtaposition of subjectivism with a bureaucratized and technical environment results in incomplete social control. The gaps within this uneven structure of control provide opportunities for intermittent autonomy and a sense of expansive possibility. Zijderveld relates these characteristics of middle-class society to the contradictions between control and alienation, on the one hand, and private autonomy and freedom on the other. Such a society controls the individual in multiple ways but without coherence and uniformity of domination.[2] Consequently, free spaces left by default are filled up with individual dreams, fantasies, desires and utopias, which impart feelings of freedom and independence. A free play of conceptuality with the potency to produce novel forms occurs within the interstices of a rationalized world.

The middle classes are ambivalently related to the structures that they create and operate but cannot fully control. These structures include centralized bureaucratic, as well as decentralized and small-scale organizations. In both types of structures middle-class specialists experience a sense of immediate control in the production of goods and services. The appearance of autonomy is enhanced by what Harvey has theorized as a fundamental reorganization of late capitalism. His analysis of the shift from Fordist to flexible accumulation points to a trend towards decreasing visibility of bureaucratic controls.[3]

For Harvey, the era of manufacturing for mass markets under the auspices of centralized corporations in a regulated economic environment, referred to as Fordism, is contrasted with decentralized small firms producing in small batches for specialized markets that is labelled flexible accumulation. As he explained it, the contraction of manufacturing in advanced capitalist societies since 1972 has been accompanied by a shift to services. Flexible subcontracting arrangements enabled small firms to provide finance, health care, education, advertising, marketing, real estate and other services to a network of firms of various sizes. The growth of subcontracting and consultancy created the appearance of decentralization while shifting and reorganizing corporate functions into tightly integrated networks. Under a regime of flexible accumulation, bureaucracy apparently receded into the background while coordinating formally independent firms. This type of economic environment generated occupational specialization that formed the underlying structure of the middle classes.

Flexible accumulation coexists with a bureaucratically coordinated division of labour. Together, these forms of organization drive the expansion of intermediate strata. Intensified differentiation among the new middle classes heightens individualism. Members of these groups engage in producing the appearance of choice and empowerment of individuals. They are also consumers of their own products and experience the world as a series of proliferating options.

The new middle classes are neither fully subordinated to capital nor fully autonomous. They are involved in directing the labour process without ownership of the resources under their control or participation in high level policy-making. Corporate downsizing has relocated members of these classes to entrepreneurship and flexible employment in small subcontracting firms. Flexible accumulation that swept away corporate paternalism, career paths, job security and other benefits has redefined the meaning of work. Work no longer provides a firm basis for personal identity. As a result, members of these strata are unable to form enduring identifications with any particular organization or occupational role. Attenuation of the connection between work and identity enables them to construct free-floating forms of identity independent of social institutions.

Unlike the Western middle classes, the shift from bureaucratic to flexible employment among the non-Western middle classes has been more recent. Dependence on state bureaucracies for employment until the 1980s and 1990s distinguishes these strata from their Western counterparts. Prior to the acceleration of global capitalism since 1989, non-Western middle-class positions, identities and forms of consciousness were strongly institutionalized in state bureaucracies infused with nationalist ideologies. These ideologies were traceable to the colonial period when Western powers reshaped the class structure of many non-Western societies. Wallerstein emphasized that the complexity of technology and the social system introduced by colonial capitalism created large and expanding middle classes in non-Western societies.[4] Intense ambivalence was generated within these classes by the juxtaposition of Enlightenment values in colonial education and nationalist ideologies that drew upon elements of local traditions. Non-Western middle classes also experienced a sense of inferiority from being perceived as substandard copies of their Western counterparts and were thus motivated to adopt nationalism as a form of cultural resistance to domination by the West. Ironically, these instances of nationalist resistance were incorporated into the bureaucratic structures set up by the colonial administrators. In the postcolonial period, members of the middle classes were able to employ these structures as an instrument of identity construction.

However, nationalist ideologies embodied in bureaucratic and state structures coexist with the intrusive presence of global capitalism. Trade liberalization and foreign investment have created opportunities for people with educational credentials to work outside state bureaucracies. Independent professionalism is now a more attractive option. The potential rewards of the free-wheeling private sector are enticing professionals away from public sector employment. State monopolies of professional expertise are being eroded. Young people no longer unquestioningly aspire to bureaucratic careers. State bureaucracies are gradually being pushed from the centre of economic and cultural life in many non-Western societies.

This is the scenario unfolding in Asia where the rise of the new middle classes, and their decreasing dependence on the state for employment, has attracted much attention.[5] The new middle classes in Asia have become less dependent on the state for employment. For example, by 1991 the private sector in Thailand employed the majority of well-educated middle-class workers, enabling them to exercise some degree of economic and political independence from the state.[6] Likewise, the new middle classes in Taiwan have overtaken the older middle classes. The latter comprised military personnel, civil servants and teachers, all of whom were directly dependent on the state for employment. Middle-class entrepreneurs in Taiwan now control a large sphere of activity that is autonomous from the state. Furthermore, white-collar workers in the Taiwanese service sector have emerged as significant figures in cultural and social development.[7]

The new middle classes that emerged in Asia during the 1990s are able to challenge bureaucratically constructed identities. The processes of identity construction in these groups are becoming detached from state structures. In their efforts to create alternative identities, they have the opportunity to promote individualistic activities that are independent of official ideologies. In particular, individuals located in the expanding service sector aligned with global capital have become influential in shaping new cultural identities. Their orientation towards the global consumer culture leads them to become less preoccupied with collective identities and more open to personal experimentation with other identities. One of these new identities concerns the transformation of religion from a symbol of state control to an individualistic search for meaning. For example, in Thailand there has been a resurgence of interest among the middle classes in Buddhist meditation, in order to 'make Buddhism meaningful to modern life, both as critique and affirmation'.[8]

Thus, in both advanced capitalist and industrializing non-Western societies, the expansion of the new middle classes has created a fluid situation that is conducive to new forms of consciousness generally identified as postmodern. The development of postmodern consciousness is breaking down the cultural categories associated with the old bureaucratic order and is reversing the spirit of disenchantment.

Entry into the Postmodern

Postmodern culture, an aesthetic of intense and fragmented experience dominated by the commodity form, is associated with the new middle classes. In this culture, the self is decentred and the subject is considered otiose. Only disconnected sensations exist. The market principle is accepted and celebrated.[9] However, this perceptual mode is not exclusive to the new middle classes because they actively produce and transmit it to members of other classes. The domination of late capitalist society by the media and the market ensures the widespread exposure of postmodern culture to all social strata. Even the older middle classes are not immune to the influences of postmodern culture.

In contemporary culture, flimsily constructed selves navigate the transition from the modern to the postmodern. Selves that have attained autonomy from various social structures experience a growing sense of potential. Ideologies of transcendence exist within a universe of proliferating signs and images. Such a universe is created and maintained by selves with an enhanced capacity for the production of novelty. Capitalism enables the release of individual creative energies to relativize all forms, structures, values and meanings.[10] Awareness of creative excess and potential destabilizes any sense of a centred self with firm boundaries. Rules and limits are obliterated. The production and consumption of an unceasing stream of novelties break down the coherence of the self. As creativity and the production of novel forms come to dominate social action, delirium is experienced as the putative ground of everyday life. A sense of relativity, disorientation and lack of moral regulation slides over the flux of perpetual newness. Innovation as an autonomous social force, driven by profit-seeking, empties the self of content and definition. Creativity as the limitless production of new forms sustains the late capitalist commodification of social life.

The rise of the commodity form has contributed to a condition of generalized desublimation. Desire becomes a transpersonal force driving the production of novelty and profligate consumption. The flow of desire towards disparate commodities corrodes the coherence of the self. The sense of integration around a well-defined set of values oriented towards world mastery evaporates into the dazzling efflorescence of the commodity form. Multidirectional desire channelled through the media and market implies an extremely diffuse condition of the self. In this way, the self becomes dispersed throughout a commodified world of objects. The free-flowing creative process released by the forces of late capitalism reinforces the power of objects. Objects take on the appearance of autonomy from human action and exert their influence on all social meanings.[11]

The advent of commodified objects undermines the Enlightenment emphasis on the self as an irreducible entity. Precarious and fragmented selves existing in a world of autonomous objects are no longer beholden to the principle of reason that activates the hegemony of the subject over the object. It is this principle that makes disenchantment possible, because the hegemonic subject comes to believe in its power to control objects as a matter of fact. By standing above objects, the subject is removed from identification with and involvement in the phenomenal world. It alone evaluates without being evaluated. But in the world dominated by proliferating objects, reason is redundant and fails to maintain the subject's centrality. Objects can reclaim their autonomy to exert influence beyond the limits of reason. The mystical dimension of objects is once again invoked to re-enchant the world.

Entry into postmodern culture is captivating because it frees the subject from the task of constantly differentiating itself from perceived objects. The convergence of the ubiquitous commodity form and unrestrained creativity overwhelms the subject's sense of itself as the arbiter of all phenomenal movements. It no longer needs to step back to evaluate the world, but merges with the objects of its creation without explicitly losing any sense of power. On the contrary, the implosion of the subject and object accelerates the power of delirium to break down all referential systems, stripping away the gloss of subjective identities and heightening the sensation of bare experience.

Destabilization of referential systems and the emergence of precarious identities in postmodern culture offer the possibility of re-enchantment. As selves appear to lose their solidity in the world of the commodified sign, the romantic tradition is resurrected to open new routes to re-enchantment. Romanticism is not incompatible with postmodern culture because it addresses the role of emotions and feelings in all experiential states.

The Romance of Irrationality

The romantic movement and its exaltation of the irrational has significantly shaped middle-class consciousness from the late eighteenth century until the present.[12] Traditionally, romanticism elevated feeling and imagination over reason. This has been witnessed in the sporadic outbursts of expressive culture in capitalist development. In all phases of capitalist development, middle-class commitment to rationality was accompanied by nostalgia for spontaneous styles of thought and action. The romantic counterpoint to capitalist rationality contributed to mystical and charismatic religious trends among the middle classes.

Romanticism in all its wide-ranging manifestations embodies the emotional, intuitive and creative aspects of the individual suppressed by instrumental rationality. The middle classes have sought to recover the loss of valued subjective experiences through movements of religious renewal. Romantic idealism expresses a diffuse religious sensibility of organic growth opposed to mechanized industrial society. It provides a rich source of religious inspiration. Romantic religious developments range from individualistic mysticism to the restoration of communitarian brotherliness. These forms of religious expression assert alternatives to capitalist values and definitions of the world.

Löwy views romanticism as 'a protest against modern capitalist/industrial civilization in the name of pre-capitalist values, a nostalgic *weltanschauung* opposed to certain key components of this civilization: disenchantment with the world, quantification of values, mechanization, dissolution of community, abstract rationality'.[13] Romantic protest against the injustices of the capitalist system is recurrent. For example, the creation of a grassroots church in Basic Ecclesial Communities in Latin America embodies a far-reaching critique of capitalism that includes broad-based mobilization of the poor and marginalized for a protracted struggle against poverty and violence. In this case, liberationist Christianity expresses a revival of emancipation without the distortions imposed by capitalist modernity.[14]

Alongside the romantic collectivism of liberationist Christianity, the romantic individualism of modern gnostic movements continues to influence middle-class consciousness. Theosophy, a well-known gnostic movement that developed in the nineteenth century, evoked nostalgia for ancient wisdom lost during the march of progress. Individualistic mystical experience, rather than social engagement and collective struggle against oppression, is the keynote of Theosophy and other forms of modern gnosticism that appeal to the middle classes. Helena Blavatsky, the founder of Theosophy, was a prominent figure who instilled in some members of the Western middle classes serious interest in esoteric teachings. Her performances of magic and shamanism and revelations of occult knowledge enabled her to summon archaic and heterodox religious traditions long consigned to the underground of Western civilization. In the shadow of triumphant nineteenth century industrialism and scientific rationality, Theosophy offered a strategy of struggle against the limits of bourgeois conventions and routines. The recovery of occultism provided a means for individual transcendence of capitalist modernity.[15]

Romantic individualism also included searches for alternatives to modernity in exotic cultures. In the view of the late nineteenth- and early twentieth-century romantics, the non-Western 'other' was free from the artifices and distortions of excessive rationality. Peripheral peoples living on the margins of, or entirely outside, Western civilization offered a wealth of meaning and symbolism to be enlisted in the romantic struggle against the arid conditions of modernity. Exotic peoples were seen to be living in sacred worlds where the whole of life was experienced as a seamless web of meaning. The persistence of these lifeworlds demonstrated to the romantics the possibility of opting out of modernity. Precapitalist ways of life negated everything romantic individualists despised about industrial capitalist civilization, and appropriation of the exotic 'other' became a strategy of their symbolic resistance: 'otherness' was fashioned into a symbol of meaningful aesthetic alternative to the apparent ugliness of modern commerce and industry. This symbolic resistance affirmed the integrity of the self in nature and meaningful lifeworlds, not only enhancing the autonomous self but also representing the development of romanticism within the Enlightenment framework.

In the nineteenth century, American and European intellectuals showed a serious interest in Asian philosophies and religions, producing an outlook that was critical of Western rationality.[16] In their view, cosmocentric Asian worldviews provided meaningful non-rational approaches to understanding existence in the world. Sir William Jones and other European Orientalists who engaged in the study and translation of Sanskrit texts made available sources for the romance of the exotic. American discovery of these translations activated further enthusiasm for Oriental art, culture and philosophy. These translations were taken up by American romantics such as Ralph Waldo Emerson and Henry Thoreau, and a group gathered around them, known as the Concord Circle. Members of this circle expressed their enthusiasm for Oriental culture by embarking on the study of comparative religion based on the Sanskrit text translations,[17] supplementing this project with the study of the imaginative poetic works of Walt Whitman and Edwin Arnold in which Indian spiritual traditions were represented as sources of timeless universal truth.

The romantics in the Concord Circle believed that their discovery of Indian spirituality could lead them to transcend the limits of Western civilization. By embracing Orientalism, they affirmed the integration of the self with nature. This version of Orientalism has proven to have enduring appeal among the educated and cosmopolitan middle classes in the United States. The Orient, as the antithesis of the accumulated dissatisfactions with modernity and conventional Christianity, continues to serve as a rich symbolic resource for the romantic struggles undertaken by the middle classes in the West.

Romantic individualism, as described above, has evolved into what Greeley referred to as 'personalism'.[18] According to Greeley, an ideology of this-worldly 'personal development, enrichment, and fulfillment' elevates the autonomous self above all social forms and restrictions. Personalism blends 'nineteenth-century liberalism, Marxism, Freudianism, and existentialism' into a frame of reference that, to some degree, has 'turned against its progenitors and become so dominant in both the elite and mass cultures that it may be viewed as almost a presupposition'. As part of the dynamic of middle-class consciousness, personalism has 'already become one of the unquestioned criteria by which other ideas, thoughts and symbols must be evaluated and judged'.[19] As Greeley saw it, disillusionment with the scientific age reinforced belief in personalism as the most immediate and reliable refuge from the dissatisfactions of industrial civilization. Mystical experiences became a more preferable goal than that of science.

Personalism and the soteriology of this-worldly fulfilment in mystical ecstasies are dependent on the romantic belief in the autonomous self. Classical romanticism exists within the Enlightenment paradigm where an autonomous self revolts against an inauthentic world of humanly constructed and distorting forms. The self is seen as dominated and repressed and its creative potential inhibited. In other words, classical romanticism can be construed as a type of individualistic reaction to the problem of alienation.

However, Jameson suggested that alienation had been transformed into the hallucinogenic exhilaration arising from the postmodern aesthetic of schizophrenia.[20] In contrast to classical romanticism, post-Enlightenment romanticism dissolves the subject into decentred, free-floating desire. A generalized schizophrenic perception of disconnected intensities occurs and releases a euphoria superseding alienation. Ecstasies of unmediated sensations are believed to obliterate the effects of alienation. Post-Enlightenment romanticism locates the romance of irrationality in a framework where linear time and the centred self have vanished. It then becomes possible to apprehend the world as an unhindered flow of psychic energies, filled with appearing and disappearing forms and dominated by the creative principle.

Human intentionality is superfluous within the post-Enlightenment romantic paradigm. The creative process of the world unfolds without reference to the subject. Poststructuralist writers, such as Jean Baudrillard, emphasize 'the power of the object' as something impervious to subjective processes.[21] Poststructuralists focus on the object is a strategy for decentring psychic energies by de-linking them from the subject, and the fragile nature of the self in late capitalism makes this a credible strategy. Attempts by poststructuralists to theorize the disappearance of the subject in relation to the object can be considered as a type of post-Enlightenment romanticism. In this type of romanticism, the world as unceasing creative production is treated as beyond reason and its categories. Post-Enlightenment romanticism thus offers the strategy of ecstatic immersion in a world of signs without referents. The symbol is submerged in the sign. Unlike the symbol, the sign does not maintain a clear distinction between signifier, signified and referent. This simply means that the sign is a self-representative phenomenon, lacking in mediatory structures and meanings. Intensification of sensation in the absence of stable meanings provides the condition for redefining ecstasy as the climax of commodification.

As subjective experience is transformed into ecstatic intensities, the old symbolic selves are annihilated and their energies transferred to commodified signs. The separation of the sign from structures of meaning and symbolic processes enables the sign to attain autonomy. Generalized commodification and the autonomous sign are the conditions for a post-Enlightenment romanticism that celebrates levels of intensity detached from institutional structures and bounded selves.

Conversely, romantic individualism continues to exist as an option for the middle classes, particularly for the older strata that are dependent on bureaucratic structures. These structures provide the limits to which rationality becomes subverted by the rebellious nature of romantic individualism. For members of the older middle classes, the symbol mediates subjective experience and imparts meaning to it. The Enlightenment romantic strategy of transcendence is possible where the symbol and the self retain coherence. Under these conditions, the world can be represented as a map. Meanings are grasped, assimilated and integrated within a self that is experienced as autonomous and reflexive. Hence, in late capitalism, re-enchantment is occurring amidst contending regimes of signification generated by opposition between the sign and the symbol.

Identities and Regimes of Signification

Symbolic identities exist in dependence on objectified structures of meaning. In Asia, these structures maintain an appearance of solidity as established traditions. Many Asian societies have adapted their traditions to capitalist modernity. The vibrancy of Asian traditions nourishes symbolic regimes of signification. Asian religions remain strongly symbolic in character.[22]

The Asian middle classes and their linkages to state bureaucracies contribute to the construction and maintenance of collective identities. Romantic individualism has not been an important influence in shaping middle-class forms of consciousness in Asia. On the contrary, the Asian middle classes employ the resources of modernity to sustain collective identities rooted in tradition.[23] These forms of symbolic activity simultaneously affirm tradition and modernity. The adaptation of tradition and appropriation of modernity are the main agenda of the Asian middle classes. Since they retain space for traditional values and symbolic exchange, they experience a less thorough process of disenchantment in everyday life.[24] The sacred in Asia is still treated with a realism that is not negated by the secular abstractions of modernity. Sacred symbols continue to pervade social life in Asia, and the strength of these symbols suggests that many state bureaucracies are able to utilize them to affirm collective identities. However, global capitalist expansion in Asia has brought the sign into encounters with the symbol.

Tension within middle-class consciousness in Asia has become more pronounced as global capitalism brings the sign into juxtaposition with symbolic regimes of signification. The emotional associations of the symbol are attenuated when symbols come into contact with a free flow of signs. As signs multiply and circulate, symbolic meanings and emotions are sustained only with greater effort. Individuals find themselves moving intermittently between enclaves of symbolic meaning and an expanding world of free-floating signs.

Unlike the symbol, the sign makes no demands for commitment. Emotional intensity in symbolic interaction is reduced as individuals become habituated to the 'coolness' of the sign. Obligatory collective identities appear optional in the universe of signs, which presents itself as the realm of unrestricted freedom. The attenuation of collective identities as the symbol encounters the sign may provoke defensive reactions of a nationalist or religious character. Exclusionary practices to reinforce social boundaries draw on symbolic regimes of signification for emotional effect. The resources of modernity are employed to carry out strategies of symbolic reinvigoration. Coercive means are brought into play to defend the symbol. Exclusive identities and monopolies of truth are pursued by arousing collective emotions that are directed towards the maintenance of symbols within institutionalized boundaries. Print and broadcasting media and state bureaucracies are mobilized in the reassertion of collective identities. Such symbolic activities contribute to continuing revitalization of collective cultural identities in Asia.[25]

However, symbolic activities rooted in syncretic religions can sustain collective identities without denying the attractions of the sign. For example, the eclecticism of some new Asian religions promotes activities that can accommodate identities in both the realms of the symbol and the sign. In other words, alternative religious beliefs and practices can nourish collective identities without explicit antagonism towards transformations activated by the sign. Tension between sign and symbol is minimal under such conditions (see Chapter 5).

Religious movements in the West are similarly engaged in symbolic activity directed towards strengthening the boundaries of collective identities[26] that are formed to counter the alienating conditions of modernity and to renew a sense of community in highly differentiated societies. However, religious defence of the symbol has been vigorously challenged by the pervasiveness of the New Age movement. Stemming from the activities of the 1960s counterculture movement, the New Age movement appears to be an intensification of the search for alternatives to modern culture. New Age activities concern what Heelas termed 'sacralization of the self'.[27] These activities focus on techniques for attaining inner awareness and include meditation, shamanism, divination, ecstatic dancing, retreats and seminars, but New Age seekers remove these techniques from traditional structures of meaning, thereby erasing their original symbolic character.

Unlike the efforts to maintain collectivist identities, the diverse manifestations of the New Age movement embrace all experiences that lead to the realization of the transparency of all social identities. The New Age movement is continuous with romanticism in its concern with authenticity and freedom, while at the same time abandoning traditional connections with symbolic regimes of signification. The transformation of symbols into signs facilitates the New Age quest for authenticity understood as the self stripped of contingent social identities. The sign is experienced as an arbitrary play of all forms and identities.

The regime of the sign enhances the fluidity of the New Age movement by not confining it to any specific context. New Age activities are flexibly conducted in secular, as well as religious, milieu. The New Age quest for authenticity is pursued across the boundaries of the sacred and the secular for efficacious results in business, health, education and other practical domains of everyday life. The aesthetic and spiritual concerns that preoccupy New Age seekers are not clearly distinct from this-worldly activities. Without differentiating the secular from the sacred, New Age techniques of power are not strictly viewed as religious in nature. These techniques are thus susceptible to absorption by signs.

Many New Age seekers are typically middle-class individuals who remain in the world of employment and consumption while seeking inner awareness and authenticity. Seminars and retreats cater to this market of spiritual seekers. New Age activities that promise self-empowerment particularly appeal to such seekers who 'consume' signs in their endeavours to acquire techniques of power. These techniques include meditative music, spiritual seminars, the enactment of rituals and alternative medical treatments. As signs, these products do not require commitment to specific beliefs, organizations, or identities. In their continuity with late capitalist consumer culture, New Age products connect the mainstream middle classes to cosmocentric worldviews originally limited to the Western religious periphery and to the 1960s counterculture movement.

The market and media as dominant social forms in postmodern culture produce commodified images that break down reality based on conventional relations between signifiers and referents. In other words, individuals have lost control of determining the nexus of meaning between signifier and referent. Rather, experience of proliferating free-floating signifiers leads to an aestheticism of radical discontinuity that disrupts the unifying sense of the past, present and future. Unlimited production of commodified images in postmodern culture so exceeds conventional systems of referentiality that meanings cannot be determined as fixed relations between the subject and object. In a perverse way, the excess of images has mitigated the tension between the subject and object by eliminating all fixed positions and boundaries. In short, the dualistic relation between subject and object appears to evaporate in this flood of images.

Ironically, excess of the image has made possible the return to a unified cosmos. The premodern cosmos was the creation of a minimally reflexive social world that took itself for granted. The image was assumed to be part of established reality and represented ritually controlled forces that connected all phenomena. The undifferentiated cosmos is paralleled by systems of self-defining or self-referential signs lacking any connection with structures of meaning. The stream of images that forms this cosmos is beyond any evaluation. No criteria for distinguishing one sign from another are possible as the sheer profusion of signs overwhelms any established system of meaning. The subject no longer confronts the world but instead, is recognized as an image existing among a multiplicity of images. It is in this vibrant arena of images that the New Age movement is able to transform symbols into signs of healing, shamanism and ritual fulfilment.

The End of Alienation

Does the advent of signs suggest that the age of alienation has come to an end? Is re-enchantment under the sign a prelude to the de-differentiation of the subject and object – the elimination of the dualistic condition that produces alienation? Murchland argued that the bourgeois propensity towards dualism was both disenchanting and alienating because the subject took its separation from the object as a natural fact and, as a result, experienced an abstract form of life.[28] Abstraction became a source of symbolic production. The subject could only make its relationship to the object meaningful by engaging in symbolic production. In symbolic production, human authorship of conceptual activity is obscured by the intensification of individualism and by the objective character of the external world. The reified products of human activity are experienced as separate from their creators and are not subject to human control. But the subject remained at the centre, the position from which all phenomena are reduced to manipulable abstractions.

Religion in the modern world accentuates these conditions of alienation because an autonomous self underpins the rational conquest of nature as well as submission to the alleged influences of higher powers. The symbolic production of faith addresses all meaning as the mirror between the rational self and divinity, but pragmatically reflects the power relationship between different social groups. Thus, the bourgeois self attempts to develop a reflexive stance towards symbolic production in order to seek *rapprochement* with the reified world. It sinks further into alienation since reflexivity generates more uncertainty about the perception of objects. The idea of the sacred comes to take on the characteristics of passive omnipresence, as reflexivity and uncertainty increase the distance between the subject and object.

The appearance of the sign in this context of alienation indicates a new order of relationship between the subject and object. Because the sign produces a scattering effect of sensations across all commodity forms, the presence of the subject is reduced by the multitudinous links developing rapidly in the expanding universe of objects. As objects proliferate, the world is transformed into 'sheer images of itself and for pseudo-events and "spectacles"'.[29] In this world, the subject is overshadowed by the radical discontinuity of free-floating signifiers that overturns all fixed meanings. The subject can no longer identify itself as a contender of meanings, since it too is a image in a universe of signs. Absorbed by the sign, the subject becomes hidden by multiple layers of free-floating signifiers and never surfaces to test its distance from the object. In this way, alienation seems to disappear into the vortex of the commodified world.[30]

Since the reality of the self is experienced through the consumption of signs, the idea of the sacred is no longer received as the transcendental object of subjective veneration. Experiential forms of empowerment replace the sense of alienation from a distant but powerful being. Direct entry into the sacred, rather than vicarious appropriations of religious meanings, constitutes the level in which the subject merges with the transcendental object as pure imagery. This is the order of re-enchantment in the middle classes as individual selves attempt to break free of the dualistic condition in order to immerse their transformed subjectivity in a magical cosmos of sublime signs. The New Age movement signals a process of re-enchantment as the end of the alienated subject locked in a protracted struggle with the object. The diversity of the New Age movement allows unimpeded movement between magical forms, unshackling subjective attitudes of distance and wariness towards the power of objects. For this reason, it is seen as a threat by established religions that occupy symbolic worlds with firm boundaries.

The symbols of these religions address the meaningfulness of the subject in search of the transcendental object, not the decentring of the subject into the sacred equivalence of all objects. The defence of the symbol accentuates the alienation of the subject, but in a way that increases fervour for union with the invariably distant transcendental object. For members of the middle classes who cling to the symbolic differentiation between subject and object, desperation to close the gap may increase the tendency to seek solutions in religious literalism. The turn to religious literalism indicates a symbolic backlash against the sign, since using texts and traditions as infallible sources of truth highlights the power of the word against the power of the image. Fundamentalism can be construed as an example of the attempt to uphold the symbol against the sign. Unlike the New Age movement, fundamentalism represents the antithesis of the commodified world because it stresses the symbolic basis of collective identities. We will examine the significance of these identities in the next chapter.

Notes

1 See Nicholas Abercrombie and John Urry (1983), *Capital, Labour and the Middle Classes*, London: Allen and Unwin.
2 Anton Zijderveld (1970), *The Abstract Society*, London: Allen Lane, p.126.
3 David Harvey (1989), *The Condition of Postmodernity*, Oxford: Blackwell, pp.125–40.
4 Immanuel Wallerstein (1983), *World System and Capitalist Civilization*, London: Verso, pp.83–6.
5 See Richard Robison and David Goodman (eds) (1996), *The New Rich in Asia*, London: Routledge.
6 Kevin Hewison (1996), 'Emerging Social Forces in Thailand: New Political and Economic Roles', in Robison and Goodman, ibid., pp.144, 154.
7 J.J. Chu (1996), 'Taiwan: A Fragmented Middle Class in the Making', in Robison and Goodman, *ibid.*, pp.210–11.
8 Suwanna Satha-Anand, (1990), 'Religious Movements in Contemporary Thailand', *Asian Survey*, 30, pp.395–408 at p.405.
9 See Hal Foster (ed.) (1985), *Postmodern Culture*, London: Pluto Press; Frederic Jameson (1991), *Postmodernism or the Cultural Logic of Late Capitalism*, Durham, NC: Duke University Press; Mike Featherstone (1991), *Consumer Culture and Postmodernism*, London: Sage.
10 Marshall Berman (1983), *All That is Solid Melts into Air*, London: Verso, pp.98–105.
11 Jean Baudrillard (1993), *Symbolic Exchange and Death*, London: Sage; and idem (1996), *The System of Objects*, London: Verso.
12 More extensive coverage of romanticism can be found in Colin Campbell (1987), *The Romantic Ethic and the Spirit of Consumerism*, Oxford: Blackwell; Raymond Williams (1971), *Culture and Society 1780–1950*, Harmondsworth: Penguin; Howard M. Jones (1974), *Revolution and Romanticism*, Cambridge, MA: Belknap Press; Dmitri Shalin

(1986), 'Romanticism and the Rise of Sociological Hermeneutics', *Social Research*, 53, pp.77–123; Jerome Christensen (1994), 'The Romantic Movement at the End of History,' *Critical Inquiry*, 20, pp.452–76.

13 Michael Löwy (1996), *The War of Gods: Religion and Politics in Latin America*, London: Verso, p.27.

14 Ibid., pp.32–93.

15 Joseph B. Tamney (1992), *American Society in the Buddhist Mirror*. New York: Garland, pp.8–14; see also Robert S. Ellwood, Jr (1979), *Alternative Altars: Unconventional and Eastern Spirituality in America*, Chicago: University of Chicago Press, pp.104–35.

16 Tamney, *American Society, op cit.*, pp.20–25, 31–2.

17 Rick Fields (1992), *How the Swans Came to the Lake: A Narrative History of Buddhism in America*, Boston, MA: Shambala, pp.55–63.

18 Andrew W. Greeley (1974), *Ecstasy: A Way of Knowing*, Englewood Cliffs, NJ: Prentice Hall, p.114.

19 All quotes from ibid.

20 Jameson, *Postmodernism, op.cit.*, p.33.

21 Jean Baudrillard (1990), *Fatal Strategies*, New York: Semiotext(e).

22 For example, see Nicholas Tapp (1993), 'Karma and Cosmology: Anthropology and Religion', in G. Evans (ed.), *Asia's Cultural Mosaic*, New York: Prentice Hall, pp.287–306. The term 'regime of signification' was introduced by Scott Lash to describe forms of cultural production: see Scott Lash (1990), *Sociology of Postmodernism*, London: Routledge, pp.4–5. Hence, symbolic regimes of signification refer to cultural production that depends mainly on the circulation of specific symbols in contrast to regimes of signs that are largely image-driven.

23 For example, see William R. Roff (1967), *The Origins of Malay Nationalism*, New Haven, CT: Yale University Press.

24 For example, see Niels Mulder (1978), *Mysticism and Everyday Life in Contemporary Java*, Singapore: Singapore University Press.

25 See Hans Dieter-Evers (ed.) (1993), 'Religious Revivalism in Southeast Asia', Special Issue of *Sojourn: Social Issues in Southeast Asia*, 8(1), pp.1–218.

26 See Orrin E. Klapp (1969), *Collective Search for Identity*, New York: Holt, Rinehart and Winston; James A. Beckford (1992), *Religion and Advanced Industrial Society*, London: Routledge.

27 Paul Heelas (1996), *The New Age Movement*, Oxford: Blackwell, pp.23–4. 96–7

28 Bernard Murchland (1970), *The Age of Alienation*, New York: Random House, p.60.

29 Jameson, *Postmodernism, op. cit.*, p.18.

30 Unlike Karl Marx who argued that the logic of alienation was found in the loss of ownership of produced commodities, we assert that commodification in late capitalism suppresses alienation by transforming the subject into a sign.

Chapter 4

Fundamentalism: Revenge of the Symbol

The re-enchantment of the middle classes not only highlights the power of the sign, but also the renewal of the symbolic power of the holy word.[1] The word of God as represented by scriptural texts has found new life in the phenomenon of fundamentalism. Fundamentalism is generally identified as a type of religious resurgence that is antagonistic to modernity, usually producing actions based on literal interpretations of the holy word for the fervent pursuit of salvationary goals. For example, Giddens defines fundamentalism as:

> ... nothing other than tradition defended in the traditional way – but where that mode of defence has become widely called into question.... [It] tends to accentuate the purity of a given set of doctrines, not only because it wishes to set them off from other traditions, but because it is a rejection of a model of truth linked to the dialogic engagement of ideas in a public space.[2]

If we take the defence of doctrinal purity as the basic component of fundamentalism, then fundamentalism is nothing more than a struggle to maintain the right to express symbolic, rather than dialogic, truth. This struggle reflects a deep contradiction in the bourgeois ideology of the twentieth century. This is an ideology of openness and inclusiveness, or one that celebrates infinite potential as an expression of individual strength under the expansion of reason. Whereas this strength is derived from a naïve desire for limitless creativity and choice, it is unable to gauge and embrace the multiple moral consequences of such desire. Within the limits of this ideology, fundamentalism comes to be seen as an obstinate defence of traditional ways, even though it is actually about the choice to defend traditional ways. Agency plays as much a role in fundamentalism as in other religious affiliations and actions, but it is not readily considered intrinsic to fundamentalism because of the widely received idea that fundamentalism is driven by the forces of tradition. Thus, fundamentalist religions are nothing more than 'traditional' religions competing with other religions in an expanding arena of religious worldviews and practices.

In the context of middle-class re-enchantment, the vital question is why have some middle-class individuals chosen to adopt the fundamentalist model of symbolic truth instead of experimenting with alternative models of religious meaning? Is there something unique about middle-class re-enchantment that makes fundamentalism a viable means for expressing the symbolic power of divinity? To answer these questions, we first need to analyse the origins of fundamentalism.

The Origins of Fundamentalism

Between the late nineteenth and early twentieth century, the term 'fundamentalism' appeared in Western public discourse, reflecting specifically the struggle between theological liberalism and evangelicalism within American Christianity. The rise of American fundamentalism as a specific defence of traditional authority has been well documented in George Marsden's widely cited book, *Fundamentalism and American Culture*,[3] which draws upon historical materials on American Protestantism to investigate American evangelicalism in the context of rapidly changing cultural ideologies. As Marsden put it, the fundamentalist reaction of American evangelicals was unique in the sense of their altered status within a space of 50 years:

> Respectable 'evangelicals' in the 1870s, by the 1920s they had become a laughingstock, ideological strangers in their own land. Their traditions, the ways they maintained them, and the ways they modified them are all understood better in the context of this collective uprooting.[4]

In what ways had these evangelicals become a laughing stock, their beliefs come to be regarded as obsolete, and their religious status peripheral to the mainstream? Marsden located the crisis of American evangelicalism in the 1870s. Up to this time, the religious authority of the evangelicals was not seriously questioned because of their influential position in American society. Indeed, they maintained working relationships with other worldviews stemming from Common Sense philosophy and Baconian and Newtonian science. It was the growing influence of Darwinian evolutionism that finally caused the rift between evangelicalism and science. Marsden identified the popular preacher, Henry Ward Beecher, as an important representative of the view that 'science could have its autonomy, and religion would be beyond its reach'.[5]

But the evangelicals' apparent break with science did not signal an unrelenting hostility against science. On the contrary, efforts were made to propound, as in the case of Beecher, the unfolding of the Kingdom of God through the revelations of scientific progress. It was a way of suggesting the superiority of eschatology over scientific knowledge.[6] For instance, the Dispensationalists emphasized scriptural infallibility by treating science as serving the goals of biblical eschatology. It implied that 'even though the Bible was not intended to teach science, God had guided even the poetic language so as to anticipate scientific discoveries.'[7]

By 1910 the evangelicals' apparent break with science turned out to be more of an attempt to coopt science. The publication of the 12-volume work *The Fundamentals* between 1910 and 1915 bore testimony to the intellectual energies devoted to the defence of scriptural infallibility. The issue concerning the authority of science was discussed with much vigour, particularly in the evangelicals' approach to science as offering compelling evidence for scriptural truth rather than displaying unfounded, speculative hypotheses that dismissed the authenticity of the supernatural and the miraculous. Marsden's description of this spirited defence of biblical authority accentuated the evangelicals' eagerness to form alliances with science as a means for demonstrating scriptural integrity: 'Without an *a priori* rejection of the miraculous, Scripture would always prove compatible with the highest standards of science and rationality.'[8]

Since *The Fundamentals* provided an important symbolic reference for the nascent fundamentalist movement, it meant that the evangelicals' position on science reflected a specific worldview that took objective knowledge as a mirror of God's mind, in order to establish the authenticity of their mission. Yet all this was taking place at a time when both the scientific and theological communities were making the transition to a new model of scientific determination that gave much weight to the role played by evolutionary causes. As Marsden put it,

> In America between 1860 and 1925 something like the general acceptance of a new perceptual model took place in both the scientific and theological communities. Non-Darwinists, of course, were ostracized from scientific circles. Similarly, the modern theological community adopted a model for truth that in effect stigmatized theologians who rejected evolutionary views as neither scientific nor legitimate theologians. The conservatives were equally dogmatic. No compromise could be made with a worldview whose proponents denied the fixed character of supernaturally guaranteed truth.... Fundamentalists, excluded from the community of modern theological and scientific orthodoxy, eventually were forced to establish their own community and sub-culture in which their own ideas of orthodoxy were preserved.[9]

Hence, fundamentalists became marginalized as liberal modernists took centre-stage in both the social and religious fields. After 1925, according to Marsden, fundamentalism lost its ground as a result of public ridicule. It was identified with anti-liberalism, anti-modernism and intolerance. By 1926, fundamentalists 'were much weakened minorities'.[10] For Marsden, the simplest explanation for the decline of fundamentalism in American Christianity was found in the growing public disparagement against its conservative and reactionary image. This was because '[b]y modernist definition fundamentalists were those who for sociological reasons held on to the past in stubborn and irrational resistance to inevitable changes in culture'.[11]

This brief summary of American fundamentalism does not do justice to the richly contextualized account of its rise and fall as provided by Marsden.

Nevertheless, the aim here is to show that Marsden's study was concerned with the meaning of fundamentalism, as the term was coined in 1920,[12] strictly in the American religious context. In this context, rival bodies of knowledge emerged to turn religious choice into a question of commitment to personal salvation based on scriptural infallibility or to secular values ushered in by the growth of bourgeois rationality. Marsden was seemingly emphatic about the role of personal choice in fundamentalist beliefs because he construed it to be vital to the maintenance of fundamentalism in a society experiencing rapid modern changes. As he put it, '[e]xactly correct belief then became proportionately more important to the movement as its social basis for cohesiveness decreased'.[13]

Even though Marsden's study seemed to give the impression that fundamentalism was largely an American phenomenon, he nevertheless alluded to the resemblances between American Protestant fundamentalism and Muslim fundamentalism. He concluded by saying:

> ... recent developments in Islam clearly demonstrate, as would surveys of other religious communities as well, that fundamentalism is not a strictly American phenomenon. It is American only in the sense that it was here that it took shape and flourished in its classic Protestant form.[14]

This statement is important because it identifies the classic model of fundamentalism in American Protestantism, which apparently forms the basis for cross-cultural comparisons with other religions. There seems to be a generalizing tendency in this statement to suggest that the anti-modern attitudes of fundamentalists cannot be confined only to America because modernity is a global phenomenon resisted by religious conservatives in other parts of the world as well. Therefore, fundamentalism can be unreservedly identified and studied in other cultures and societies.

About a decade separates Marsden's work and the massive project on fundamentalism organized by Martin Marty and Scott Appleby.[15] In this decade, fundamentalism was codified as a worldwide phenomenon alleged to be discernible in the fervent resistance of various groups and movements against modernization. For example, Marty analysed American fundamentalism as 'a force of resentment against "intellectuals", "elites", "the media" ... [and] people who are at home with modernization and care little for the presumed traditions'.[16] Compare this with Marty and Appleby's description of global fundamentalism some seven years later:

> fundamentalists begin as traditionalists who perceive some challenge or threat to their core identity, both social and personal. They are not frivolous, nor do they deal with peripheral assaults. If they lose on the central issues, they believe they lose everything. They react, they fight back with great innovative power.[17]

The underlying character of fundamentalism, as seen in Marty's analysis of the American variety, pertains to a deep-seated antagonism against the symbols of modernity. When this character is extrapolated to the world stage, it seems to take on a greater sense of desperation because of the higher stakes involved in religious competition. The sense of ambivalence in American fundamentalism towards modern technology, suggested by Marty's reference to its utilization by fundamentalists as a type of borrowing, is also evident in religious fundamentalism in other parts of the world. Thus, by the 1990s, fundamentalism was no longer a word of American usage; it had become an epithet for a specific religious reaction against modernity all over the world. As Marty and Appleby claimed, 'fundamentalism is here to stay ... If the term were to be rejected, the public would have to find some other word if it is to make sense of a set of global phenomena which urgently bid to be understood.'[18]

What makes fundamentalism a global concern these days is its alleged relation to the violent means by which religious goals are achieved. Martin suggested that it was the 1978 Islamic revolution in Iran that 'helped to create a market for expertise in fundamentalism'.[19] From this perspective, fundamentalism was no longer considered a trivial matter concerning obsolete or irrational worldviews held by isolated communities of religious traditionalists, but was seen to be closely associated with the systematic means for bringing about changes in institutional authority and administration. It is the fear of these changes as a reversal of modernization on a massive scale that has made expert 'knowledge' of fundamentalism indispensable for religious and political counteractions. One may even speak of a growth in the fundamentalism industry to convey the sense of urgency among liberal modernists to clarify, describe and analyse the apparent upsurge of religious militarism in many communities around the world today.

For Marty and Appleby, this task involved the identification of 'family resemblances' among fundamentalist groups and movements around the world. This entailed comparison of fundamentalist beliefs and actions across a broad spectrum of religions, namely Judaism, Islam, Protestantism, Catholicism, Hinduism, Sikhism, Theravada Buddhism, Confucianism and Japanese new religions. They asserted that '[a]dherence to an inerrant scripture is not, for example, a central feature of each of the groups studied. But there do seem to be "family resemblances" among these movements, though they spring from different religious traditions and geographical regions'.[20]

When we compare this statement with the description by Marsden on the scriptural infallibility of Protestant fundamentalism in America, we see a shift in meaning, as the term is no longer solely concerned with the authority of the holy word but with other behavioural characteristics, such as opposition to modernity. Family resemblances, in this case, provide a convenient and parsimonious approach to outlining what Marty and Appleby called the 'ideal typical impulse' of fundamentalism of which there are at least seven components: religious idealism, dramatic eschatologies, contra-acculturative orientation, missionary zeal, crisis of identity, ideological selectivity, and charismatic appeal.[21]

In the last decade of the twentieth century, Western scholars did not appear to take lightly the resilience of fundamentalist endeavours. For example, Marty and Appleby spoke of contemporary fundamentalism as 'both derivative and vitally original' and as promoting religious identity based on 'a recreated political and social order'.[22] It is as though advocates of fundamentalism – many of whom are educated members of the middle classes in their own societies[23] – do not find the effects of bourgeois rationality convincing or plausible. Instead, they attempt to renew faith in their scriptural traditions to nullify the claims of modernity.

The beginning of the twenty-first century does not seem to witness the mitigation of fundamentalist fervour. It is the constant challenge presented by religious traditionalism to Western bourgeois rationality that has created a sense of urgency among the defenders of modernity to reify the notion of fundamentalism. As Martin expressed it, '[The Fundamentalism] project seeks to reify a notion born of North American Protestantism and raised to the level of public policy discourse by the growing incidence of religious movements that express antisecularist and anti-Western worldviews'.[24] To delve into the reification of fundamentalism is to understand the contradictions of liberalism and middle-class reactions to these contradictions.

The Crisis of Liberalism

There are two aspects of liberalism that need to be examined – namely, philosophical liberalism and liberal democracy. Both are based on the logic of rational individualism developed during the period of the Western Enlightenment. This logic, promoting the unfettered sovereignty of discrete selves, emerged from the pens of European philosophers who saw freedom as an unconditional mitigation of traditional influences and, more specifically, the removal of established church authority.

Bertrand Russell asserted that philosophical liberalism

> ... was the product of England and Holland, and had certain well-marked characteristics. It stood for religious toleration; it was Protestant, but of a latitudinarian rather than of a fanatical kind; it regarded the wars of religion as silly. It valued commerce and industry, and favoured the rising middle class rather than the monarchy and the aristocracy; it had immense respect for the rights of property, especially when accumulated by the labours of the individual possessor.[25]

Based on this viewpoint, liberalism led to an ideology of acquisitiveness that not only sought to weld individual might with the contingencies of capitalism, but also to open political doors to the bourgeoisie and non-aristocratic contenders for power. In this respect, liberalism invented the conditions of egalitarian participation in order to promote better opportunities for business and political transactions.

The development of liberal democracy in Western Europe and North America rested on the ideology that people everywhere sought individual rights, private ownership of property, rational dialogue and natural law. Representation of this ideology in the writings of Locke, Bentham, Mill, Spencer and others suggests the historical specificity of their interests, but its avid defence in recent years by Fukuyama implies a greater striving to universalize its ideology, which was aided by the decline of socialism and communism around the world.[26]

The paradox of liberalism is that it attempts to convert the privileges of the few into the rights of the many, and in the process encounters contradictory developments that challenge its premises. For example, Groth remarked that:

> ... people have a right to petition their government. Democratic constitutions generally guarantee this. But what about the efforts of lobbyists who, thanks to their superior financial resources or personal connections, make the wishes of a few people count for more with the legislators or the bureaucrats than those of perhaps untold millions.[27]

In recent years these contradictions have become more acute with the emergence of poststructuralism and postmodernism, both of which may be regarded as the rebellious offspring of liberalism. Poststructuralism was a special creation of French intellectuals in the wake of the May 1968 protest movement in Paris. As described by Seidman, it 'combined the disruptive gesture of existentialism, the high-minded seriousness of structuralism, and the political engagement of Marxism...to demonstrate that all claims to identify an order to society, knowledge, or morality were unwarranted and concealed a will to power'.[28] While poststructuralism and postmodernism are bonded by several themes related to difference, fragmentation, heterogeneity and indeterminacy, postmodernism seems to have flourished on its own as a form of cultural change in the West with significant reorganization of perceptions in history, art, architecture, literature and the social sciences.[29]

The emergence of these critical perspectives has increased liberalism's sensitivity to its own defence and renewal. New concepts such as 'communicative action', 'reflexive modernization', and 'dialogic democracy' were introduced to open the way for renewing liberal modes of mutual understanding and consensual interaction.[30] In the attempt to renew liberalism, fundamentalism came to be defined as a new symbol of irrationality. It was identified as an anachronistic way of defending particular traditions, even to the point of violence. The dispute between liberal Protestants and evangelicals in American Christianity became the *locus classicus* of the controversy over fundamentalism. The controversy was gradually extended beyond the borders of the United States to affect global discourse concerning the conflict between liberalism and traditionalism.

Shupe and Hadden noted that:

> ... the concept fundamentalist was not applied to any non-Christian group until the Islamic revolution in Iran in 1979.... Fundamentalist leaders in the United States were...infuriated with the application of the concept to Muslims, for it suggested that the Ayatollah Khomeini and New Christian Right leaders like Jerry Falwell were fanatical 'brothers under the skin'.[31]

It was American reaction to the Iranian revolution and the taking of US citizens as hostages, reinforced by powerful images from the US mass media, that activated the reification of fundamentalism. In a sense, the extrapolation of American Protestant fundamentalism to Iranian Shiite activism transformed the crisis of liberalism into a global concern with the threat of religious extremism.

As a result, fundamentalism is defined as a syndrome specifying the unfolding of eschatological defence, scriptural rigidity and religious militarism over time. The unfolding of this syndrome has now come to be defined as part of the globalization process – in fact, the term 'global fundamentalism' has entered the vocabulary of the social sciences.[32] To show how fundamentalism has been reified as a global religious syndrome requiring intellectual and practical attention, we will examine its apparent manifestation in three non-Christian religions: Islam, Sikhism and Japanese new religions.[33]

The Muslim Dilemma

Muslim belief in Muhammad as the last messenger of God and in the pure essence of the Qur'anic revelations has made Islam a unique religious force in the modern world. As an exemplar of uncompromising revelatory beliefs, Islam maintains a defensive posture against modernity because it seeks to uphold the Qur'anic revelations in the context of advancing global markets, liberal politics and secular actions. Yet, Muslims around the world have not rejected modernity in its entirety; many of them have incorporated modern technology, democratic ideologies and capitalist innovations in their daily lives. Nevertheless, it is the symbolic encounter of Islam with modernity that has raised the issue of fundamentalism in the reshaping of Muslim identity in the late twentieth and early twenty-first centuries.

The obsession with this symbolic encounter and its outcomes seems to have influenced the sociological interpretation of Islam's future, particularly the sociopolitical conditions that allegedly produce fundamentalism. This is an interpretation that focuses on 'the crisis of modern Islam'. According to

Bassam Tibi, a Muslim sociologist, the crisis of modern Islam resulted from economic impoverishment of the Muslim population and cultural conflicts over westernization.[34] By economic impoverishment he meant the industrial exploitation of raw materials that has brought about disparities in incomes and living standards. In the case of the Middle East, the discovery of oil at the beginning of the twentieth century, and its subsequent exploitation, transformed traditional tribal societies into wage labour economies. In Saudi Arabia, Tibi claimed, 90 per cent of the population at the beginning of the twentieth century was engaged in agricultural activities, but by the end of the 1970s this figure had declined to 33 per cent. A large proportion of peasants and bedouins entered the wage labour market as unskilled workers in the oil industry. Many foreign workers were imported as skilled labour. This division of labour implied a wide divergence in wages and standards of living and therefore became a source of social unrest for the uprooted peasants and bedouins. Such a situation was ripe for the renewal of Islam.

Tibi explained that westernization followed on the heels of European colonialism in the Middle East. Western educational institutions introduced into Muslim societies created an intellectual elite that could not relate to indigenous cultural values and thereby became alienated. In Tibi's words:

> The Westernization of education produced Arab intellectuals whose Westernized secular norms and values were no longer Islamic. Today these secular ideologies, unable to fulfill their visionary promises, are suffering an acute crisis. And it is out of this crisis, when both social and political legitimacy have been cast in doubt, that the repoliticization of Islam has sprung.[35]

Tibi himself made a plea for the secularization of Islam, by which he meant the attenuation of religious beliefs and practices in a larger social system premised on modern developments. However, he found that many Muslims misunderstood the meaning of secularization, often equating it with promiscuity and notions of cultural degeneracy. Similarly, Fatima Mernissi, a Moroccan sociologist, voiced her reservations about the meaning of modernity, individualism and secularism in Muslim societies:

> With a few rare exceptions (notably Turkey), the modern Muslim state has never called itself secular, and has never committed itself to teaching individual initiative. On the contrary, individualism always held a rather ambiguous place among the 'reformers' of the nineteenth-century nationalist movement. This movement, focused on the struggle against colonization and therefore virtually anti-Western, was obliged to root itself more deeply than ever in Islam.... The Muslim past they reactivated did not anchor modern identity in the rationalist tradition. In fact, the nationalists were prisoners of a historical situation that inevitably made modernity a no-win choice. Either they might construct modernity by claiming the humanistic heritage of the

> Western colonizer at the risk of losing unity … or they could carefully safeguard a sense of unity in the face of the colonizer by clinging to the past … and foreclosing all Western innovation.[36]

Mernissi addressed the intense ambivalence experienced by Muslims in their attempt to hold on to a religious tradition that promised salvation and, at the same time, become progressive by imbibing modern values that conflict with that tradition. Akbar Ahmed described this situation most succinctly as a complex, love–hate relationship between Muslims and the West, particularly the United States: 'From being the nearest thing to paradise on earth, the USA became the Great Satan…. It holds Muslim society in thrall.'[37]

What these Muslim social scientists are saying is that modernity has become excruciatingly painful for Muslims because of the difficulties in reconciling two sets of symbols. The symbols of modernity are highly prized for their association with the meaning of human progressiveness and self-determination. But Islamic symbols are still highly charged with prophetic charisma. Rapid industrial development and economic disparities are likely to trigger a conflict between these symbolic systems, and cause a reversion to traditional religious beliefs as a defence against the intrusion of modernity.

Muslim concern about the impact of modernity on their religious system has become a major characteristic of Muslim fundamentalism. The large body of works by Western writers on Muslim fundamentalism has made the term part of everyday language. The term has also become a code word for religious irrationalism, extremism and violence because of its association with specific Muslim political events of the 1970s and 1980s. The urgency to control this perceived religious threat is complemented by the need to understand its origins and development. Recent studies of Muslim fundamentalism attempt to explain its emergence in eighteenth- and nineteenth- century Islamic reformism, such as the Wahhabi movement of eighteenth-century Arabia and the Mahdi movement of Muhammad Ahmad in nineteenth-century Sudan that later 'provided fundamentalism with sophisticated modern vocabulary for the defense of Islam'.[38] At the same time, the emergence of nationalist, anti-imperialist sentiments transformed religious fervour into a concerted effort to preserve Islamic traditionalism in the face of the modern secular state. The rise of the Muslim Brotherhood was one such reaction.

In recent years, the appearance of Osama bin Laden, the Saudi dissident, and his al-Qaeda movement has come to represent a formidably well-organized form of Islamic resistance against Western interests in the Middle East. Suspecting Osama to be the mastermind behind the bombing of US embassies in Kenya and Tanzania in 1998, and the devastating attacks on the World Trade Centre in New York and the Pentagon in Washington DC in September 2001, US officials demanded his surrender from the Taliban government of Afghanistan which had given him sanctuary. The Taliban's refusal to accede to the US demand triggered a highly complex conflict that not only involved the intercession of American military forces in the ongoing Afghan civil war, but also heightened the fear of 'global terrorism' possibly launched by Muslim dissidents in various parts of the world.

The confrontation between Islamic fundamentalism and Western secular interests, exemplified by Osama's resistance against US power, appears to resemble the fulfilment of Samuel Huntington's prediction in his well-known work, *The Clash of Civilizations*. However, the complex divisions within the Muslim world raise many issues that cannot possibly justify the clash between Islam and the West as inevitable. One of these issues relates to the question of Islamic reformism in the context of global modernization. In Afghanistan, reformism was not undertaken by the Taliban as a direct challenge to global modernization, but as a systematic way to consolidate political and cultural relations in war-torn society. It was the conjunction of the Taliban's reformist ideals and Osama's anti-imperialist objectives that this particular fundamentalism came to be perceived as a grave threat to Western security.

The explanation of Islamic reformism as underlying the growth of Muslim fundamentalism is ostensibly a discourse on the behavioural and ideological reactions of Muslims to a rapidly changing world in which they seemed to exercise little control. This suggests that a certain type of social failure provides the catalyst or causal condition for reformism and, later, fundamentalism to become a reality characterized by ideological rigidity, social frustration and spiralling violence. Thus, Lawrence affirms the nature of such a reality by commenting on the inability of the Muslim elite to bring to realization a better future in the concluding decades of the twentieth century:

> It is the vision of the dispossessed that drives a certain class of male elites. Most are not only urban but upwardly mobile: whether educated in modern universities of the Islamic world or EuroAmerica, they have become scientifically professionalized. One may characterize them as fervently Qur'anic, patriarchal, ascetic, and anti-Western, but they are, above all, unemployed or underemployed. Whether frustrated engineers, disaffected doctors, or underpaid bureaucrats in meaningless public jobs, potential Islamic fundamentalists are *petits bourgeois* in search of a purpose from the meaningful past to preempt the uncertain future.[39]

Even some Muslim scholars have come to accept the argument that Islamic fundamentalism is a function of specific social conditions related to modernization. For example, Saiedi attributed the rise of Islamic fundamentalism to 'a situation of sociological anomie'.[40] Manzoor argued that the 'fundamentalist vision of the ideological Islamic state ... arose as a response to the power of the West'.[41] Rahman asserted that 'neo-fundamentalism is basically a function of laymen, many of whom are professionals – lawyers, doctors, engineers'.[42] Indeed, the reality of Islamic fundamentalism appears to thrive in the context of an ambivalent relationship with modernity. Muslim fundamentalists are often represented as antagonistic towards the spread of modern values and worldviews, but at the same time they are described as somewhat partial to the products of modernity. For instance, Pipes explained fundamentalism as attracting Muslims who were initially open to modern secularism, but later faced many problems resulting from modern dilemmas.[43]

It is this ambivalence that makes Islamic fundamentalism a feared phenomenon because the oscillation between explicit rejection and implicit admiration of Western achievements does not seem to offer any sense of stability to the notion of Muslim identity. Yet, this apparent lack of stability is also the source of strength for Muslim identity, since it is the political actions of Muslim fundamentalists that direct the attention of the West to Islam. But there are writers who want to dismiss this form of religious strength as undesirable because they construe Islamic modernism as a more viable alternative. For example, Ahady suggested that Islamic fundamentalism was apparently on the decline by the end of the 1980s. He took this to mean that Muslims actually desired to 'combine Islamic identity and values with elements of modernization' and that 'Islamic modernism does not make headlines like Islamic fundamentalism, [but] it is a very serious ideological alternative in the Islamic world'.[44]

Thus, the reification of Islamic fundamentalism is only possible in a context of conflict conceptualized as an inevitable clash between two irreconcilable civilizations: Western and Islamic. This clash tends to be represented as an outcome of the time lag between the two civilizations, the West being more 'developed' in terms of its secular transformation compared to Islamic culture that is ostensibly embedded in a traditional eschatology. Fundamentalism in Islam is, therefore, logically an activation of a defensive posture to uphold an eschatology that is not immediately compatible with the ideals of modern secularism. Yet, there are attempts by some scholars of Islamic society to argue against the meaning of fundamentalism in the mainstream historical tradition of Islam. For example, Asad asserted that Islamic zealotry is a product of the modernizing state, particularly in the state's 'project of transforming the totality of society and subjectivity in the direction of continuous productive progress, that creates a space for a correspondingly ambitious Islamicist politics. Islamic history had no such space. That space, with its totalitarian potentialities, belongs entirely to Western modernity.'[45]

In all these constructions of Islamic fundamentalism, modernity is pivotal to the meaning of the Islamic struggle – as though Muslims live under a terrible strain from their encounter with the West. Similarly, Muslims who seek some form of *rapprochement* with the West also find it difficult to ignore the 'excesses' of Islamic fundamentalism, as though religious irrationalism is always threatening to tar Muslim extremists and liberals with the same brush. From these virtual expressions of religious angst, the notion of Islamic fundamentalism becomes ensconced in the cultural and political vocabulary of both the Western and Islamic world. It is the 'bogeyman' of a religious tradition that is still trying to come to terms with the power of Western modernity. It is also a symbol of religious power that is continuous with prophetic charisma and Qur'anic revelations.

The Politics of Sikh Identity

Unlike the Islamic experience, Sikh fundamentalism is not so much concerned with modernity as it is with religious identity and ethnic separatism in the Indian subcontinent. The problem of religious and cultural identity has been central to the social formation of the Sikh community. What has been described as Sikh fundamentalism is related to a complex case of radical Sikh resistance to the Indian nation-state, developing from the internal politics of Punjab and influencing the perceptions and actions of Sikhs in other parts of the world.[46]

The basic components of Sikh identity are found in their external appearance (turbans, unshorn hair, and the five Ks[47]), the tradition of the 10 gurus, and the holy scripture (the Guru Granth Sahib). Yet there are certain aspects of Sikh narratives and codes that complicate the self-evident nature of Sikh religious, regional and linguistic identity. Sharma has examined the problematic nature of Sikh identity by comparing various accounts concerning Hindu and Muslim influences on Sikhism.[48] In particular, he referred to writings that identified Guru Nanak, the founder of Sikhism, as primarily Hindu or Islamic in outlook, acknowledging also the strongly presented view in other accounts that Guru Nanak was neither of these. He concluded that Sikh identity was largely a function of politics in Punjab: 'The root of the Sikh crisis lies in the fact that Sikh identity cannot find full political expression even within the truncated Punjab.'[49]

On the other hand, Oberoi argued that Sikh fundamentalism reflected Sikh efforts to organize and unify cultural opinion on a standard of behaviour. According to him, Sikhism lacked an established clergy and tradition that defined orthodoxy. Instead, there were 'different subtraditions evolving within Sikhism, each claiming allegiance and constituents for its own version'.[50] In other words, Sikh fundamentalists have a genuine concern about the ambiguity of their social, cultural and legal codes. Without a proper definition and organization of these codes, the question of Sikh identity becomes difficult to manage and is subjected to contesting viewpoints. Hence, Sikh fundamentalists have demanded the institutionalization of Sikh personal law not unlike that found in Islamic *shari'a*.[51]

Since Sikh fundamentalism is alleged to be the expression of an identity problem, its reification in political terms seems to be associated with the rise of Jarnail Singh Bhindrawale, a charismatic Sikh preacher, and his violent confrontation with the Nirankaris, a reprobate sect in Sikhism, in Amritsar in 1978. According to Oberoi, many observers have dated the emergence of Sikh fundamentalism to this event.[52] They treat Sikh fundamentalism as a recent phenomenon that arose from sectarian problems in Punjab. However, Madan maintains that Sikh fundamentalism is not as recent as it seems, but can be traced to the cultural activities of the tenth guru, Gobind Singh, who sanctioned the practice of righteous war and introduced the custom of Sikh baptism.[53]

Undoubtedly, there is a general agreement on the reactive nature of Sikh fundamentalism, but not on the critical moment of its appearance. This simply means that there is a sense of arbitrariness in the way Sikh fundamentalism is pinpointed for emphasizing its apparently growing threat to Punjab and India as a whole. Such reification has become possible not only because of the mass media, but also because of the spread of the Sikh population to other parts of the world. The global connections of Sikh organizations have made the problem of Sikh identity more acute because standard references to orthodoxy are no longer simply determined by a single body in one location. Furthermore, the Sikh diaspora implies that Sikhs have the option to choose their organizational allegiances. The question of Sikh fundamentalism is complicated by personal choice in a situation of competition for loyalty to different sets of norms. For example, in North America today there are efforts by Sikhs 'to routinize Sikhism as "a monolithic, codified and reified religion" with universal norms of orthodoxy and orthopraxy'.[54] Sikhs in the West tend to consider themselves as authentic representatives of Sikh orthodoxy, while the Punjabi Sikhs dismiss them as outsiders.[55] The struggle over Sikh orthodoxy suggests that the meaning of Sikh fundamentalism cannot be separated from a contested tradition now no longer confined to Punjab.

From Shinto to Secularization

It is not difficult to imagine how the political actions of Muslim and Sikh radicals have been reified as fundamentalism. Yet, the application of this term to Japanese new religions seems somewhat out of place because the political radicalism found in Islam and Sikhism is either lacking or given different expressions in the Japanese case. Davis reported that:

> ... [the] word *fundamentalism* seems a bit incongruous in the Japanese setting. If one were to ask a group of perceptive foreign visitors to describe the essence of Japanese life, the word 'fundamentalist' probably would not even come to their minds.... Specialists on Japanese religion and society seldom, if ever, use the word. The Japanese themselves usually reserve the words *konponshugi*, *genrishugi*, or the English loan-word *fuandamentarizumu* for Iranian or Protestant fundamentalism or for the Korean Unification Church.

This means that for most Japanese, to be a 'fundamentalist' is to be a devotee of a *foreign* religion.[56]

Nevertheless, Davis applied the term to Japanese politics and various new religions because he treated it 'as a powerful theoretical concept in the comparative sociological study of religion and politics'.[57] He found 'in Japan a tendency to deal with complex social and political realities by withdrawing symbolically to the imagined simplicities of the past – a tendency that can be called fundamentalist'.[58] However, in his conclusion he maintained that religious fundamentalism has not generally prospered in Japan, although political fundamentalism was a more significant possibility. The reason for this conclusion can be found in his discussion of the state's appropriation of Shinto (Japan's indigenous religion) for political purposes. Towards the end of the nineteenth century, the Meiji government attempted to transform Shinto shrines into symbols of patriotism, taking control of the priesthood and appointing official scholars to announce the conditions of religious practice through Imperial Rescripts. This came to be known as State Shinto. This type of religious nationalism defined Japanese political fundamentalism until the end of the Second World War. Despite the collapse of State Shinto after 1945, Davis contends that political fundamentalism in Japan is very much alive, as evidenced by the growth of about 800 right-wing organizations with a total membership of approximately 120 000 throughout the country.[59]

This fundamentalism is extrapolated to the activities of the new religions, which 'seem to have originated as a reaction to the growing complexity and frustration of Japanese life'.[60] But Davis recognizes that the resentment and frustration underlying the fundamentalism of the Japanese new religions are not similar to the characteristics of the classical fundamentalism of American Protestantism, such as the notion of scriptural infallibility. In the case of the Soka Gakkai, one of Japan's most popular new religions, he described it as 'perhaps opportunistic rather than fundamentalistic'.[61]

Davis's analysis of fundamentalism in Japan may be considered ambiguous because it is not clear whether such an analysis can be applied without reservation in analysing the connections between religion and politics in Japan. Some of the major works on Japanese new religions hardly ever used the term 'fundamentalism' to describe and explain religious change in Japan; they principally focus on social and religious anomie in post-war Japan as an explanation of the rise of new religious movements. These movements are believed to provide a ready outlet for the sense of aimlessness experienced by a population that is no longer under the direct influence of State Shinto or any form of religious orthodoxy. For example, McFarland explained that attraction to these religions was a response to endemic social change, particularly the upheavals caused by urban migration and defeat in the war.[62]

The problem of anomie continues to be cited as central to understanding the emergence of the *Shinshinshukyo* (neo-new religions) of the 1970s and

1980s. For example, Metraux in explaining the appeal of Aum Shinrikyo to younger Japanese said that '[i]t offered members a way out of the anomie of modern Japan'.[63] This movement gained a certain notoriety in the history of Japanese new religions when, in March 1995, its members allegedly released deadly sarin gas on three Tokyo subway lines resulting in 12 deaths and thousands of injuries. Even Davis has referred to this movement as a 'criminal religion' rather than a type of fundamentalism.[64]

All these works are concerned with the conditions in postwar Japan that have given birth to a large number of new religious movements, yet none of these relates their emergence to fundamentalism. In fact, Noda argued that 'Japan has no clearly recognizable orthodoxy corresponding to Sunni Islam, and thus a fundamentalist movement advocating return to a specific orthodox religion is unlikely to arise'.[65] He suggested that secularization made possible the application of the Religious Juridical Persons Law which guarantees 'maximum freedom to conduct religious activities for religious organizations of all kinds, large and small, regardless of their nature or practices'.[66] As a result, no one religious group is said to be ahead of, or preferred to, others in terms of ethical standing. In other words, secularization has evened out religious choice in an environment that is 'overly pluralistic and mutable'.[67] In such an environment, religious organizations and movements may confront civil authorities, but this confrontation is not perceived as a challenge from fundamentalist groups. Rather, it is a confrontation that occurs in what Noda called a religious limbo where 'the majority of Japanese do not distinguish between orthodox and heterodox religion'.[68]

Thus, it is not easy to reify fundamentalism in a country like Japan because social and cultural conditions do not favour the classification of religious actions into central and marginal types, especially since the decline of State Shinto after the Second World War. Modernization in Japan has heightened identity problems linked to the idealized *furusato*, the imagined homeland allegedly wrecked by the chaos of modern life.[69] Under these conditions, traditional and new religions compete without explicit reference to an orthodox model.

Symbols of Resistance

The application of the term 'fundamentalism' to Islam, Sikhism and Japanese new religions illustrates the reifying powers of a project that attempts to universalize the notion of doctrinal absolutism and its unrelenting defence in an age of sweeping modern changes. Indeed, the picture that emerges from this project to compare fundamentalism around the world is replete with images of closed-mindedness, paranoia, inflexible cognition and unrepentant hostility towards the outside world. It is as though fundamentalists are people who await Armageddon within the imagined safety of their religious cocoon while the modern world passes them by. In the words of Marty and Appleby,

> Fundamentalism has appeared as a tendency, a habit of mind, found within religious communities and paradigmatically embodied in certain representative individuals and movements, which manifests itself as a strategy, or set of strategies, by which beleaguered believers attempt to preserve their distinctive identity as a people or group. Feeling this identity to be at risk in the contemporary era, they fortify it by a selective retrieval of doctrines, beliefs, and practices from a sacred past.... [R]eligious identity thus renewed becomes the exclusive and absolute basis for a recreated political and social order that is oriented to the future rather than the past. By selecting elements of tradition and modernity, fundamentalists seek to remake the world in the service of a dual commitment to the unfolding eschatological drama... and to self-preservation.[70]

Undoubtedly, such a representation of fundamentalism would not be accepted by fundamentalists because this representation is a product of a rationality that distinguishes between objective comprehension of, and subjective involvement in, religious actions. The former position distances the observer from the sacred lifeworld and may result in reservations about fundamentalist beliefs. The latter, on the other hand, suggests an 'irrational' perspective because emotionally charged believers are purportedly not expected to make good unbiased observers. These believers are practitioners whose sacred worldviews dictate their actions. Yet, they cannot be considered insensitive to the world around them. In other words, they may regard their fundamentalism as a source of stability in a modern world that is continuously changing and in crisis.

For the fundamentalist, the sacred lifeworld represents a sphere of stability and security. It is purportedly not subjected to the upheavals and uncertainties of modernity because it has no open-ended future but one grounded in an eschatological reality. The fundamental belief in this reality provides a sense of guardedness against other realities that emphasize change as a constant. Hence, modernity as a reality of dynamic change undermines the belief in a sacred lifeworld guaranteeing consistency, equanimity and regularity. For this reason, fundamentalists tend not to consider modernity as inherently superior to their worldviews since modern values acknowledge the element of instability in change.

Central to this sacred lifeworld is a set of general beliefs in the attainment of a religiously wholesome community in which stability is manifested and enjoyed. A brief comparison of some fundamentalist movements reveals the commitment of the movements' members to achieve the conditions in which this stability is completely realized.

Gush Emunim or the Bloc of the Faithful in Israel, emerged in the mid-1970s as a Jewish movement that 'became the self-proclaimed herald of the re-Judaization of Israel, over against a state and a society culturally dominated by a secular and a quasi-socialist conception of Zionism'.[71] The sacred lifeworld of the Gush Emunim focused on the reclamation of the whole land of Israel as biblically conceived in the covenant between God and the Jews as the chosen people. The process of re-Judaization was not simply confined to the assertion of Israeli sovereignty over the whole land of Israel but also included the revitalization of Jewish religious identity. As Aran explained it,

> At the forefront of the battle to expand Israeli colonization and extend Israeli sovereignty over the Territories, [Gush Emunim] is essentially striving to win hearts and minds, to include more Israelis within its own version of Judaism. The compulsive preoccupation with the exact location of international boundaries is simultaneously an attempt to negotiate and ultimately eliminate the boundaries between secular and observant Jews. Thus, the desire to erase the Green Line and control the whole Land of Israel is also a desire for a 'complete' Judaism which would transcend the differences between the religious and secular worlds.[72]

This 'complete' Judaism, therefore, offers a sense of belonging and stability thought to have been lost for thousands of years, but now on the verge of being attained with the reclamation of Jewish lands and religious identity. It is this goal of stability that drives Gush Emunim members in the sense that they would no longer have to suffer the iniquities of being outsiders in other societies or of being separated from a single common identity. The objective of gaining this stability is clearly revealed in Aran's remarks that '[Gush Emunim] perceives settlement in Judea and Samaria not only as restoration of the Zionist spirit but also as *tikkun* – the kabbalistic concept of healing, repairing, and transforming the entire universe'.[73]

Similarly, the emergence of the Rashtriya Svayamsevak Sangh (RSS) in the 1920s and its continued influence in India today mark an important chapter in the nationalist drive towards the formation of a unified Hindu community. Along with other Hindu nationalist organizations, the RSS is able to draw from the vast corpus of traditional Hindu scriptures, philosophies and laws to promote a specific vision of the Hindu nation. Gold summarized this vision succinctly:

> The Hindu Nation envisioned by the RSS would live in the subcontinent as an ordered organic whole. This vision is in many ways consistent with traditional views of caste hierarchy, where different castes serve complementary functions; but as is often the case in moderate Hindu reform, the RSS ideal of caste is revised to emphasize all functions as *equal* in the sense of being necessary for the social organism.[74]

This vision embodies a particular form of religious stability related to an organic pattern of caste functions, which seemingly does not contradict the idea of social integrity and harmony.

Finally, Theravada Buddhist movements in Sri Lanka and Thailand also appear to manifest the same pattern of striving towards a stable core in the midst of rapid modern changes in society. In Sri Lanka, the revival of Buddhism from the time of Dharmapala in the late nineteenth century to the rise of the Janata Vimukti Peramuna in the 1970s has taken on the form of a Sinhalese nationalism that attempts to restore a particular religious order. According to Swearer:

> In the cosmology of Sinhalese Buddhist nationalism, non-Sinhalese Buddhists are maintained in hierarchic subordination to Sinhalese Buddhists. The integrity of the state therefore is dependent on its capacity to maintain by the exercise of its power the hierarchical interrelation of all those it encloses. In terms congenial to Buddhism: when the *Buddhadhamma* (the truth represented by the Buddha's teaching) is opposed, chaos results, the hierarchic social order is compromised, the principle of encompassment is attacked, and demonic forces are unleashed.[75]

Swearer also treated the emergence of two Thai Buddhist movements – the Dhammakaya and Santi Asoka – as responses to 'religious and cultural confusion' as well as 'decline abetted by rampant modernization and secularization'.[76] These two movements offer meditation and specific ethical lifestyles for attaining a sense of Buddhist unity and stability assumed to be in jeopardy in this day and age.

A comparison of these three examples suggests that one would be hard-pressed to find any irrationalism in the movements' objective of recovering the nucleus of religious stability said to be lost in the chaos of modern times. It is clearly unrealistic to deny that some fundamentalist movements have been involved in militant actions, but such actions do not necessarily represent *in toto* the sacred lifeworld idealized and pursued by the movements' members. Such actions, on the other hand, may be regarded as a type of strategy for resisting the modern condition of living in a multi-ethnic and multireligious world. In the eyes of many fundamentalists, this condition cannot possibly provide the stability of the sacred lifeworld they desire. Resistance may come to symbolize the movements' efforts to preserve their members' existence in a righteous order in opposition to the goals of modernity perceived by them as ephemeral and illusory.

In the decades following the end of the Second World War, the study of religious resistance was not specifically identified as an empirical investigation of fundamentalism.[77] During that time, the problem of religious resistance was overshadowed by the struggle between the forces of liberalism and socialism in the Cold War. Religious resistance in different parts of the world did not seem to make a global impact because the question of survival was determined primarily by the politics of the Cold War and not by the preservation of sacred lifeworlds. All this changed in the late 1980s following the collapse of the Soviet Union and the reunification of Germany. Suddenly, the spectre of the Cold War was over and the project of modernity could continue under the liberal auspices of Western Europe and the United States. But the religious challenge to modernity became more visible because sacred lifeworlds came to represent the remaining sphere of values that would not easily succumb to the juggernaut effects of a new world order led by the liberal West.

Under these changed conditions of world politics, the defence of sacred lifeworlds came to be defined as a rise in religious fundamentalism associated with acts of fanaticism, violence, and terrorism. Fundamentalism was no longer an exclusive term of reference to a form of biblical defence and resistance in American Christianity. It came to connote a type of danger stemming from religious rigidity and unswerving loyalty to traditional values embedded in a sacred lifeworld. For example, in the case of Islam Esposito argued that:

> ... [the] West often reinforces the equation of Islam with danger or threat, viewing the Islamic world with catchwords like 'militant Islam,' 'Islamic fundamentalism,' and 'terrorism.' Our selective memory then blocks our ability to appreciate the other side of the equation – the sources of Muslim images of the West in turn as the 'real' threat to them.[78]

The triumph of liberalism gave the impression that the 'end of history' would bring about a realization of individualistic and democratic values and put to rest all forms of collectivist ideologies constraining the creative potential of individuals. It elevated the role of the middle classes in activating these changes. As suggested in the preceding chapter, the middle classes formed the vanguard for restructuring capital and culture in the new global order. Members of these classes determined the direction of social change in an era of reduced ideological competition and unimpeded creativity. Yet, the perceived threat of fundamentalism contradicts the expectations underlying the triumph of liberalism, especially in the light of middle-class participation in the defence of sacred lifeworlds. As a form of resistance to liberalism, middle-class involvement in fundamentalism accentuates the problematic nature of liberalism's own unfolding after the end of the Cold War.

The crisis of reflexivity, outlined in Chapter 1, reflects the implosive effects of liberalism's triumph. Without challenges from communism and socialism, liberalism's internal logic has unravelled to produce a paradoxical relationship between freedom and scepticism. The unrestrained capacity to accumulate experience and knowledge is also the source of increasing doubt about the meaning of knowledge. As heirs of this paradox, members of the middle classes are exposed to the dissonance arising from the deepening crisis of reflexivity. For some members of the middle classes, the search for a solution to this crisis resulted in a return to traditional beliefs that seemed to guarantee some form of stability. In particular, the notion of scriptural infallibility provided a means for overcoming the uncertainty of individualistic freedom in an era that witnessed the defeat of collectivist ideologies. Scriptural infallibility implied a sacred lifeworld that was predetermined by providence and so could not be subjected to the fluctuations of human reflexivity.

Commitment to the sacred lifeworld and defence of scriptural realities characterize some of the choices available to disillusioned members of the middle classes in search of alternatives beyond the liberal paradigm of freedom and progress. For these members, the pursuit of scriptural realities not only symbolizes resistance to liberalism, but also denotes the attempt to disprivilege the assumptions of modernity. In other words, they want to deconstruct the boundaries that lead to the compartmentalization of modern life. By this action, religious symbols are made indistinguishable from cultural, political and economic symbols.

The fundamentalist attempt to restore a holistic definition of religion and society suggests a strategy not unlike that found in postmodernism. At first glance, there appears to be no common ground between postmodernism and fundamentalism. Postmodernism contains an underlying strand of nihilism, and the relativity of values and the dissolution of a fixed viewpoint are recurrent themes within it:[79] thus, it represents a view without viewpoints. On the other hand, fundamentalism stresses a viewpoint based on scriptural literalism, sacred values or millennarian expectations. Fundamentalism seems to be diametrical to postmodernism because it is emphatically antinihilistic and religiously foundational. There are no stranger bedfellows than postmodernism and fundamentalism. Indeed, both are interlocked in an ironic relationship to challenge the meaning of modernity.

Yet, fundamentalism shares with postmodernism the tendency towards de-differentiation or actions that challenge the artificiality of boundaries between phenomena, fields of specialization and the products of human endeavour. This characteristic comprises the fundamentalists' and postmodernists' opposition to modernity. In this regard, postmodernism is specifically a movement of decentring that attempts to disparage the centrality of a subject in the interpretation of phenomena. It advocates the removal of subject-centred methodology and the breakdown of the distinction between subject and object. Conversely, fundamentalist de-differentiation does not represent a movement of decentring because it is concerned with a renewed meaning of life under the centre of divine power. Fundamentalists reject the necessity of special boundaries for making religion alien to other spheres of life.

Despite this difference between postmodern and fundamentalist de-differentiation, the search for holism provides a key to understanding the symbols of resistance to the fragmented experience of modernity and the uncertainties of the neo-liberal era. Postmodernism lacks the puritan commitments of fundamentalism, but its deconstructive approach can be used to privilege fundamentalism's attempt to empower the continuity between religion and society. This simply means that fundamentalism is not judged as an aberration of modernity, but as its own movement for actualizing the religious in the social and vice versa. From this perspective, fundamentalism can be addressed as a possible transcendence of, rather than a mere role, on 'a stage that [fundamentalists] did not construct and which they cannot destroy'.[80]

The Challenge of Signs

The triumph of liberalism coincides with the trend of re-enchantment, resulting in a proliferation of religious choices that opens up a new spiritual landscape for the twenty-first century. Fundamentalism is just one of many choices that suggest the reappearance of charisma in a situation of attenuated political ideologies. Since Cold War political symbols no longer dominate the international scene, religious symbols come to play a more active role in the search for an ideal and stable lifeworld. Fundamentalism not only thrives on such symbols, but also advances the display of textual charisma as a hegemonic representation of a better world to come. For disillusioned members of the middle classes, such symbolic display comes to be seen as an attractive choice in a world overcrowded with failed political symbols.

The fundamentalist attempt to hegemonize the world of symbolic truth has not gone unchallenged. Re-enchantment in the post-Cold War era is also characterized by the regime of the sign. As argued in the previous chapters, the proliferation of signs has transformed the religious field into marketed arenas of salvation. Unlike the symbol, the sign does not mediate sources of sacred power: it is both the vehicle and experience of sacred power, providing religious seekers with immediate access to realms of re-enchantment. These seekers may come from the middle classes, but they are not specifically attracted to the salvationary symbols of fundamentalism. Rather, they are more inclined to explore the innovative dimensions of religious signs as a celebration of the increased freedom of the individual in the neo-liberal era. Instead of demarcating and defending sacred lifeworlds, they pursue signs that lead to novel religious experiences.

To what extent are middle-class seekers influenced by signs rather than by symbols? Would fundamentalist movements be overshadowed by the increasing influence of the sign? While fundamentalism has come to symbolize traditionalistic opposition to modernity, the contradictions of liberalism have propelled disaffected members of the middle classes to discover alternative ways that are receptive to traditional forms of religion without reducing individualistic freedom. These alternative routes to new sacred identities blend elements of traditional religion with innovative interpretations of spiritual consciousness. The individual seeker is free to choose from the expanding field of new religious styles and practices. The development of the Internet has increased individual freedom for exploring religious innovations, exposing each seeker to the power of the sign.

As digital culture comes to influence all aspects of people's lives around the world, signs will be expected to exert dominance over symbols. Such a scenario does not imply the end of fundamentalism. The symbols of fundamentalism continue to provide support to middle-class individuals seeking re-enchantment through established traditions and scriptures. But fundamentalism is not responsive to market conditions that are currently obliterating old symbols or turning them into fodder for the system of signs. Under these conditions, fundamentalism may gradually be overshadowed by new spiritual identities that thrive on reinvented traditions in an era of rapid technological changes. The emergence of New Age shamanism exemplifies the transformation of traditional religion in the culture of signs. It offers re-enchantment in a marketplace of relentless innovation. We will explore this marketplace in the next chapter.

Notes

1 Some of the arguments in this chapter first appeared in a paper presented by the first author at a conference on fundamentalism sponsored by the Institute of Malaysian and International Studies and the Friedrich Naumann Foundation, and held in Kuala Lumpur, Malaysia, April 1996.
2 Anthony Giddens (1994), *Beyond Left and Right*, Cambridge: Polity Press, p.6.
3 George M. Marsden (1980), *Fundamentalism and American Culture: The Shaping of Twentieth-Century Evangelicalism, 1870–1925*, New York: Oxford University Press.
4 Ibid., p.vi.
5 Ibid., pp.20-21.
6 Ibid., p.24.
7 Ibid., pp.56-57.
8 Ibid., p.121.
9 Ibid., p.215.
10 Ibid., p.191.
11 Ibid., p.185.
12 Ibid., p.119.
13 Ibid., p.205.
14 Ibid., pp.227-228.
15 See Martin E. Marty and R. Scott Appleby (eds) (1991), *Fundamentalisms Observed*, Chicago: University of Chicago Press; idem (1992), *Fundamentalism and Society*, Chicago: University of Chicago Press; idem (1993), *Fundamentalisms and the State*, Chicago: University of Chicago Press; idem (1994), *Accounting for Fundamentalisms*, Chicago: University of Chicago Press; idem (1995), *Fundamentalisms Comprehended*, Chicago: University of Chicago Press. Other volumes dealing with global fundamentalism include Lionel Caplan (ed.) (1987), *Studies in Religious Fundamentalism*, Albany, NY: State University of New York Press; Jeffrey K. Hadden and Anson Shupe (eds.) (1989), *Secularization and Fundamentalism Reconsidered*, New York: Paragon House; Lawrence Kaplan (ed.) (1992), *Fundamentalism in Comparative Perspective*, Amherst, MA: University of Massachusetts Press; Bruce Lawrence (1995), *Defenders of God: The Fundamentalist Revolt Against the Modern Age*, Columbia, SC: University of South Carolina Press; Gilles Kepel (1994), *The Revenge of God: The Resurgence of Islam, Christianity and Judaism in the Modern World*, Cambridge: Polity Press; Mark Juergensmeyer (1993), *The New Cold War: Religious Nationalism Confronts the State*, Berkeley, CA: University of California Press.
16 Martin E. Marty (1984), 'Fundamentalism as a Social Phenomenon', in G.M. Marsden (ed.), *Evangelicalism and Modern America*, Grand Rapids, MI: Eerdmans, p.66.

17 Martin E. Marty and R. Scott Appleby, 'Introduction – The Fundamentalism Project: A User's Guide', in M.E. Marty and R.S. Appleby (eds), *Fundamentalisms Observed, op.cit.*, p.ix.
18 Ibid., p.viii.
19 Richard C. Martin (1994), 'Review of *Fundamentalisms Observed* and *Fundamentalism in Comparative Perspective*', *History of Religions*, 34, pp.194–6 at p.194.
20 The Fundamentalism Project Newsletter (1989), p.1.
21 Marty and Appleby, *Fundamentalisms Observed, op.cit.*, pp.817–33.
22 Ibid., p.835.
23 See Lawrence,*Defenders of God, op.cit.*, pp.212–3, 216; Kepel, *The Revenge of God, op. cit.*, pp.124-125.
24 Martin, 'Review', *op.cit.*, pp. 195–6.
25 Bertrand Russell (1961), *History of Western Philosophy*, London: Allen and Unwin, pp. 577–8.
26 Francis Fukuyama (1992), *The End of History and the Last Man*, New York: Free Press.
27 Alexander J.Groth (1971), *Major Ideologies*, New York: Wiley, p.56.
28 Steven Seidman (1994), *Contested Knowledge*, Oxford: Blackwell, pp.201–2.
29 See Margaret A. Rose (1991), *The Post-Modern and the Post-Industrial*, Cambridge: Cambridge University Press.
30 See Jürgen Habermas (1984, 1987), *Theory of Communicative Action*, 2 vols, Boston, MA: Beacon Press; Ulrich Beck, Anthony Giddens and Scott Lash (1994), *Reflexive Modernization*, Cambridge: Polity Press; Anthony Giddens (1994), *Beyond Left and Right*, Cambridge: Polity Press.
31 Anson Shupe and Jeffrey K. Hadden (1989), 'Is There Such a Thing as Global Fundamentalism?', in J.K. Hadden and A. Shupe (eds), *Secularization and Fundamentalism Reconsidered*, New York: Paragon House, p.110.
32 Ibid., p.111.
33 Since fundamentalism was first identified as a phenomenon in American Christianity, it would seem logical to examine its emergence in other religions as claimed by sociologists and other scholars of religion. We have selected these three religions for comparison because two (Islam, Sikhism) have received inordinate attention in the media and Japanese new religions have not received such attention before.
34 Bassam Tibi (1988), *The Crisis of Modern Islam*, Salt Lake City, UT: University of Utah Press.
35 Ibid., p.50.
36 Fatima Mernissi (1992), *Islam and Democracy*, Reading, MA: Addison-Wesley, p.42.
37 Akbar S. Ahmed (1988), *Discovering Islam*, London: Routledge, p.217.
38 John O. Voll (1991), 'Fundamentalism in the Sunni Arab World: Egypt and the Sudan', in Marty and Appleby (eds), *Fundamentalisms Observed, op.cit.*, p.356.
39 Lawrence, *Defenders of God, op.cit.*, p.197.
40 Nader Saiedi (1986), 'What is Islamic Fundamentalism?', in J.K. Hadden and A. Shupe (eds), *Prophetic Religions and Politics*, New York: Paragon House, p.193.
41 S. Parvez Manzoor (1991), 'The Future of Muslim Politics: Critique of the 'Fundamentalist' Theory of the Islamic State', *Futures*, 23, pp.289–301 at p.293.
42 Fazlur Rahman (1981), 'Roots of Islamic Neo-Fundamentalism', in P.H. Stoddard, D.C. Cuthell and M.W. Sullivan (eds), *Change and the Muslim World*, Syracuse, NY: Syracuse University Press, p.34.
43 Daniel Pipes (1989), 'Fundamentalist Muslims in World Politics', in Hadden and Shupe, *Secularization and Fundamentalism Reconsidered, op.cit.*, p.125.
44 Anwar-ul-Haq Ahady (1992), 'The Decline of Islamic Fundamentalism', *Journal of Asian and African Studies*, 27, pp.229–43 at p.241.

45 Talal Asad (1997), 'Europe Against Islam: Islam in Europe', *The Muslim World*, 87, pp.183–95 at p.190.
46 See T.N. Madan (1991), 'The Double-Edged Sword: Fundamentalism and the Sikh Religious Tradition', in Marty and Appleby, *Fundamentalisms Observed*, *op.cit.*, Chapter 10; and Harjot Oberoi (1993), 'Sikh Fundamentalism: Translating History into Theory', in Marty and Appleby, *Fundamentalisms and the State*, *op.cit.*, Chapter 12.
47 The five Ks are *kesa* (unshorn hair), *kanga* (comb), *kara* (steel bracelet), *kachh* (short breeches), and *kirpan* (sword).
48 Arvind Sharma (1988), 'The Sikh Crisis in India: A Question of Identity', in A. Shupe and J.K. Hadden (eds), *The Politics of Religion and Social Change*, New York: Paragon House, pp.190–203.
49 Ibid., p.200.
50 Oberoi, 'Sikh Fundamentalism', *op.cit.*, p.271.
51 Ibid., p.271.
52 Ibid., p.273.
53 Madan, 'The Double-Edged Sword', *op.cit.*, p.617.
54 Verne A. Dusenbery (1989), 'Of Singh Sabhas, Siri Singh Sahibs, and Sikh Scholars: Sikh Discourse from North America in the 1970s', in N.G. Barrier and V.A. Dusenbery (eds), *The Sikh Diaspora*, Delhi: Chanakya Publications, p.93.
55 Ibid., pp.96–7.
56 Winston Davis (1991), 'Fundamentalism in Japan: Religious and Political', in Marty and Appleby, *Fundamentalisms Observed*, *op.cit.*, Chapter 14, pp.783–4.
57 Ibid., p.784.
58 Ibid., p.805.
59 Ibid., p.793.
60 Ibid., p.797.
61 Ibid., p.804.
62 H. Neill McFarland (1970), *The Rush Hour of the Gods: A Study of New Religious Movements in Japan*, New York: Harper Colophon Books.
63 Daniel Metraux (1995), 'Religious Terrorism in Japan: The Fatal Appeal of Aum Shinrikyo', *Asian Survey*, 35, pp.1140–54 at p.1149.
64 Cited in *ibid.*, p.1142.
65 Nobuo Noda (1996), 'Apocalyptic Cults and Japanese Religiosity', *Japan Review of International Affairs*, 10, pp.116–27 at p.121.
66 Ibid., p.122.
67 Ibid., p.126.
68 Ibid., p.123.
69 Ian Reader (1991), *Religion in Contemporary Japan*, London: Macmillan, pp.237–9.
70 Martin E. Marty and R. Scott Appleby (1991), 'Conclusion: An Interim Report on a Hypothetical Family', in Marty and Appleby, *Fundamentalisms Observed*, *op.cit.*, Chapter 15, p.835.
71 Kepel, *The Revenge of God*, *op.cit.*, p.140.
72 Gideon Aran (1991), 'Jewish Zionist Fundamentalism: The Bloc of the Faithful in Israel (Gush Emunim)', in Marty and Appleby, *Fundamentalisms Observed*, *op.cit.*, Chapter 5, p.295.
73 Ibid., p.292.
74 Daniel Gold (1991), 'Organized Hinduisms: From Vedic Truth to Hindu Nation', in Marty and Appleby, *Fundamentalisms Observed*, *op.cit.*, Chapter 9, p.553.
75 Donald K. Swearer (1991), 'Fundamentalistic Movements in Theravada Buddhism', in Marty and Appleby, *Fundamentalisms Observed*, *op.cit.*, Chapter 11, p.650.
76 Ibid., p.656.
77 For example, Bryan Wilson (1973), *Magic and the Millennium*, New York: Harper and Row, 1973, in studying religious movements of protest around the world used the term

'sectarianism' rather than 'fundamentalism'. The latter term appeared no more than five times in a text of over 500 pages.

78 John L. Esposito (1992), *The Islamic Threat: Myth or Reality?*, New York: Oxford University Press, p.171.

79 For a comprehensive ontological treatment of postmodernism, see Keith Tester (1993), *The Life and Times of Post-Modernity*, London: Routledge.

80 Lawrence, *Defenders of God*, *op.cit.*, p.227.

Chapter 5

The Renewal of Shamanism

The immanent power of charisma surfaces in the revival of shamanism. An undifferentiated and monistic cosmos is embodied in shamanic practices that enable full participation in the unfolding of phenomena. As the most archaic of religious practices, shamanism makes the web of cosmic connections concretely present in, and inseparable from, charisma. Communication between the visible and invisible worlds has been pursued in a broad range of human societies that include paleolithic hunting bands as well as high-tech societies.[1] Shamans connect these worlds through their ability to engage in ecstatic experience. Mastery of shamanic techniques enables movement between ordinary and non-ordinary states of consciousness. The power obtained from these techniques cannot be monopolized, since it is universally accessible to anyone who attains proficiency in shamanic practices.

The institutionalized role of the shaman in premodern societies seemingly centres charisma in the activities of certain individuals. However, the confinement of ecstasy to structured settings is always transitory and subject to competition from individuals who unexpectedly experience non-ordinary states of consciousness. Unauthorized experiences of other realities may be publicized, interpreted and organized, thus subverting institutionalized monopolies of ecstasy. No finality or closure can ever be effectively imputed to ecstatic experience. It remains a possibility open to individuals irrespective of what social milieu may circumscribe their choices and activities. Shamanic ecstasy is generally a more available option in stateless, tribal societies where decentralized forms of social power provide more space for seeking and recognizing the significance of visionary experience.

On the other hand, centralized state structures tend to be hostile towards shamanic ecstasy. Resistance to bureaucratic control, nevertheless, flourishes on the margins of societies where ecstatic experiences are discouraged and disparaged. Religious cults and movements may spring from such resistance that embraces visionary experiences together with organized forms of rebellion.[2] In other words, charisma grounded in individual experience of other realities cannot be decisively excluded from any form of social life.

In modern Asia, shamanism persists as an indispensable means of solving problems in everyday life. In the postmodern West, shamanism is being reinvented as an extension of the human potential movement.[3] It is this movement that has located the self as the abode of untapped powers and capacities. For individuals involved in this movement, awareness of the protean self as the site of ecstatic experience opens the way for charisma to manifest. However, not every individual seeker knows the techniques of ecstasy or succeeds in mastering them. But the possibility of non-ordinary experience, exemplified by the shaman, provides a fertile source of new religious messages that offer consciousness expansion, self-discovery and fulfilment of human potential. These messages demonstrate to the seeker the possibility of accessing charismatic experiences in an organized way that connects them with cosmic forces. The proliferation of shamanic religious movements in the United States expresses the ubiquity of charisma in a highly rationalized society renowned for its technological achievements.[4]

The purpose of this chapter is to show that shamanism is undergoing significant changes in the West and Asia, particularly in the way in which it manifests charismatic power under the regime of symbols or signs. We first begin with an analysis of New Age shamanism.

New Age Shamanism

Widespread experimentation with hallucinogenic drugs on the part of middle-class Western youths in the 1960s created an awareness of alternative realities. Extraordinary mental states experienced through such drugs provided a glimpse of shamanic worlds to individuals tied routinely to industrial capitalist lifestyles. Hallucinogens especially attracted those seeking vibrant holistic experiences; they enabled ordinary people unrestrained access to visionary experience generally restricted to special individuals. They heightened interest in visionary experience has led educated middle-class individuals to study and appreciate anthropological accounts of shamanic peoples.

Anthropological documentation of hallucinogenic plant use by shamans in tribal societies was seen to inspire middle-class exploration of alternative realities.[5] Middle-class interest in shamanism was directed towards the discovery and release of the protean self. Novel experiences were sought for their value in enhancing consciousness and in freeing the self from institutional controls. Shamanic techniques were appreciated as means not only for erasing the boundaries between the self and the phenomenal world, but also because they were believed to transform the self into a sacred object within a monistic cosmos.

In recent years some academics in the West have attempted to teach shamanic techniques to the public. Among the academic cultural brokers who packaged shamanic experiences for middle-class consumers were Carlos Castaneda and Michael Harner, both of whom graduated with doctorates in anthropology from reputable American universities. They moved from the representation of shamanism in symbolic lifeworlds to the enactment of shamanism in an emerging culture of signs. In the culture of signs, experiences produced within exotic lifeworlds can be formulated as popular manuals of practice. The dissemination of these experiences through cassette tapes and seminars has aided the middle-class search for cultural alternatives. The role of academic cultural brokers in the reinvention of shamanism can therefore be studied as part of the process of re-enchantment in the West.

Carlos Castaneda and Michael Harner wrote highly personalized accounts of shamanism as practised by indigenous peoples of the Americas, which went beyond the viewpoint of the detached observer. They used the rational structures of bourgeois society – the university in particular – to demonstrate to the educated middle classes the possibility of transcending ordinary consciousness. Their participation in the cultures of shamanic peoples captured the imagination of middle-class romantics. While their abandonment of claims to objectivity disturbed their professional colleagues, their elimination of distance between the professional anthropologist and the exotic 'other' enhanced the relevance of their writings to many New Age seekers.

The dissolution of the boundaries between subject and object embodied in their writings made possible the emergence of academic shamans in the New Age movement. The academic shaman is a skilful cultural broker who simultaneously represents the rational intellectual and the primitive 'other' in the quest for knowledge. As rational intellectuals, Castaneda and Harner temporarily entered into the lifeworlds of shamanic peoples to explore forms of consciousness found beyond the industrial capitalist milieu. The knowledge they sought dissolved the objectivity that structured their academic roles and disciplines. Only by allowing their personal being to be incorporated into the culture of their subjects could Castaneda and Harner attain intuitive shamanic knowledge. Having returned from their intense and extraordinary journeys, they spoke as shamans, rather than aloof observers, in representing shamanic experience and practice.

Castaneda and Harner collapsed the boundaries between anthropology and shamanism, freeing themselves from the limited role of merely representing shamanism for elite intellectual consumption. They proceeded to present their personal experiences with a beguiling immediacy that invited audience participation. Their experiences were depicted as expressing human potential that is directly available to interested seekers from any walk of life. In disclosing specific shamanic techniques, they conveyed the message that anyone can take up shamanism for purposes of self-development and consciousness expansion.

The Way of the Sorcerer

Who was Carlos Castaneda? He was a Peruvian immigrant to the United States who studied anthropology at the University of California, Los Angeles, and wrote his masters and doctoral theses on his apprenticeship to Don Juan Matus, a Yaqui shaman. These two academic works were turned into bestsellers in the late 1960s and early 1970s. Following his literary success, he wrote several more books on his shamanic adventures.[6] His writings were not immediately accepted as authentic by many members of the anthropology profession and controversy raged over his work mostly in the 1970s and for part of the 1980s.[7] Nevertheless, despite criticisms of his work, he attracted a large public following. In the early 1990s he introduced to the public a physical discipline called 'Tensegrity' that he claimed was based on certain movements practised by the shamans of ancient Mexico. He died in Los Angeles in 1998.

The last word has yet to be written on Castaneda as an anthropologist and shaman. Despite professional scepticism of his standing as an ethnographer, the metaphorical truth of Castaneda's works has been far more compelling to his readers and admirers than the issues concerning Don Juan's authenticity raised by his critics. His books have sold millions of copies worldwide. To many New Age seekers, Castaneda is regarded as an important guru who opened the door to other realities. What is it about his writings that have beguiled so many readers? We will examine his claims in the context of re-enchantment in the West.

Castaneda began his research on shamanism in 1960, a few years before the countercultural movement began in earnest. It was as though his research became a harbinger of the radical changes in American society that produced advocates of hallucinogenic experiences. He began his research with an attempt to collect information on medicinal plants used by Sonora Indians. An introduction to an old Yaqui Indian *yerbero*, a gatherer and seller of medicinal plants, in a town on the Arizona-Mexico border led him to undertake an apprenticeship in sorcery spanning a 14-year period. This apprenticeship, under the old Yaqui, Don Juan Matus, was a process of desocialization whereby his rational thought was relentlessly dismantled. Forceful experiences of other realities induced by Don Juan's 'power plants' weakened his perceptions of the common-sense world and increased his receptivity to non-ordinary consciousness.

Castaneda's apprenticeship to Don Juan entailed learning an alternative description of the world. Don Juan insisted that this kind of learning could only occur when Castaneda's common-sense world collapsed. He imparted his teachings by deliberately deceiving and frightening Castaneda on various occasions. At other times, he induced confusion or laughter to dispel Castaneda's smug intellectualizing. Knocked off balance when subjected to these experiences, Castaneda began to loosen his grip on the certainties which his socialization had instilled in him. The undoing of his socialization provided him with an ongoing demonstration of how worlds were constructed and deconstructed. It enabled him to attain a degree of detachment and control. Consequently, Don Juan inspired him with the ideal of becoming a sorcerer or a man of knowledge, which overtook his initial objective of writing an academic thesis.

For Don Juan, sorcery was not just the acquisition of personal power, but also the attainment of impeccability, or detached decisiveness born of mental clarity. Having freed himself from the taint of the conflicting emotions and motivations that dominated an ordinary person, the sorcerer was said to be able to execute impeccable actions without a second thought. Don Juan taught Castaneda that a sorcerer used his knowledge to acquire power and was prepared at all times to confront whatever forces arose internally or externally, treating every encounter with these forces as his final battle. There was no room for questioning or intellectualizing; only confident and unhesitating action gave the sorcerer the possibility of victory in his struggles.

Castaneda's apprenticeship radically changed his attitude towards the common-sense world. He began to perceive the rationality that formed the background of bourgeois consciousness in relative terms. Don Juan's sorcery did not require an outright rejection of common-sense rationality but only detachment and distancing from it. What Castaneda attained in his apprenticeship was an understanding of rationality as a partial description of the world that coexisted with other partial descriptions. Assimilation of Don Juan's teachings by Castaneda and his readers undermined the tyranny of absolutism.

Alongside the disorienting experiences with hallucinogenic plants, Castaneda was introduced to the control of dream states as a gateway to shamanic power.[8] The dream is a fundamental vehicle of visionary experience and power in numerous shamanic traditions. As a direct source of shamanic power, dreaming enables the aspiring shaman to accumulate sufficient power to attain the continuity of consciousness that unfolds into intuitive knowledge. In Don Juan's teachings, the sorcerer could act deliberately in dreams by selecting items that imparted power and then manipulating them to produce practical results. Power to discover things that were concealed and to control events experienced in waking consciousness was obtained through this kind of deliberate action. Castaneda learned from Don Juan that the first step to acquiring shamanic power was to 'set up dreaming' – that is, to gain awareness of being in the dream state and of one's capacity to exercise pragmatic control over the general situation experienced in the dream, similar to the control of any activity in waking consciousness.

Don Juan instructed Castaneda to set up dreaming by looking at his hands in his dreams.[9] He went on to draw Castaneda's attention to the fluidity of dream objects. As the dreamer looked at objects, they changed shape. The dreamer had to learn not only to look at things but also to maintain focus on them. Dreaming became real when everything was brought into focus. When this was accomplished the boundaries between sleeping and waking consciousness dissolved: there was no difference between action performed while sleeping or while waking. However, the stabilization of dream images required a high degree of mental control. For example, when the hands in the dream began to change shape, the dreamer was instructed to immediately shift focus to another object and then to return to the hands again. The aspiring sorcerer gained power as he perfected this technique of stabilizing dream images.

After more than ten years of apprenticeship, Castaneda acknowledged being very much a beginner in the art of dreaming. However, Don Juan's indigenous apprentices were trained in the art of dreaming from the beginning of their tutelage. So, by the time Castaneda met them, they were highly accomplished.[10] Don Juan gave these apprentices the responsibility of completing Castaneda's training in dreaming. During training, he learned that the female apprentices were the most proficient dreamers and under their direction, dreaming provided him with a gateway to shamanic power.

In the early 1980s Castaneda claimed the status of a fully-fledged sorcerer and the successor to Don Juan. He became known as the *nagual* – the leader of a group of apprentice sorcerers.[11] The new *nagual* was an exemplary teacher, adept in manoeuvring between multiple realities. He continued his mentor's shamanic tradition without abandoning the practical rationalism and resources of bourgeois society. At the same time, he stepped beyond his writings to create a charismatic movement that included commercial organizations to promote shamanic products for a mass market of seekers.[12]

Castaneda was able to reach the public through these organizations with his practice called 'Tensegrity'. Taking the architectural principles of tension and integrity, the term 'Tensegrity' was coined to label the modern version of physical movements allegedly developed by Mexican shamans in the era preceding the Spanish Conquest. Castaneda described these movements as an extension of the art of dreaming.[13] The extraordinary states of physical prowess and well-being experienced during conscious, controlled dreaming could be reproduced through performance of the bodily movements known as 'magical passes'. According to Castaneda, the shamans of ancient Mexico regarded 'magical passes' as their most precious knowledge, which they taught only to their initiates in strict secrecy. Don Juan had maintained this ancient tradition in teaching the 'magical passes' only to his disciples. However, in the early 1990s Castaneda and the remaining disciples decided to abandon the secrecy surrounding the 'magical passes', in the interest of making the ancient knowledge widely accessible to the public.[14]

The 'magical passes' were packaged as team demonstrations at seminars and also as videotapes. Castaneda's special appearances at 'Tensegrity' seminars were a strong drawing point, attracting hundreds of participants.[15] Originating in the personal charisma of Don Juan, 'Tensegrity' has become a growing movement of practitioners autonomously pursuing freedom of perception.[16]

The decision to break with the tradition of secrecy and to teach shamanic practices through a mass movement marks a definitive shift from the romantic, countercultural spirit of the 1960s to the sign-filled markets of the 1990s. The transformation of Don Juan's shamanic teachings into an urban, middle class movement resonates with the mass marketing of the human potential movement in the 1990s. Like the youthful admirers of Castaneda in the 1960s who sought escape from the clutches of bourgeois rationality, participants in 'Tensegrity' also attempt to effect cognitive changes by learning the 'magical passes' that reputedly transcend ordinary reality. However, middle-class youths influenced by the countercultural values of the 1960s gravitated toward Castaneda's writings not only as a form of self-discovery, but also as a symbol of freedom from the iron cages of modernity. This symbol of freedom appealed to a readership that had ceased to find relevance in Judeo-Christian teachings. For them, salvation was not taken as the eschatological redemption found in Judeo-Christian teachings, but the complete realization of human potential exemplified by Castaneda's shamanic experiences.

In the 1990s, Castaneda's writings were still relevant to many middle-class seekers but were disseminated in a sign culture of expanding cultural products. In this culture, total well-being and awareness are dealt with pragmatically without firm symbolic attachments. It is this pragmatism that weakens the symbolic boundaries between self and social structure, allowing the power of the masses to flourish under market conditions. The appearance of 'Tensegrity' at this time suggests that Castaneda's personalized apprenticeship to Don Juan, organized around traditional shamanic symbols, had now given way to another form of shamanism that thrives on commodified signs. Even after Castaneda's death, 'Tensegrity' courses were continued under the supervision of qualified instructors.[17] This development implies that New Age shamanism, organized around the production of signs, is able to respond effectively to mass markets.

The Way of the Healer

Unlike Castaneda, Michael Harner approached shamanism more as a form of holistic healing than as a specific technique of power acquisition. He first encountered shamanism as a graduate student conducting field research on the Jivaro, an indigenous people inhabiting the Amazon rainforest in eastern Ecuador. As in the case of Castaneda, Harner's research originally concerned the indigenous use of hallucinogenic plants. At first, he did not participate in the Jivaros' consumption of *ayahuasca* (Banisteriopsis caapi), a hallucinogenic vine widely available in their territory, but instead was concerned with the symbolic meanings of Jivaro shamanism. It was on later field trips that he joined his informants in shamanic rituals involving the ingestion of *ayahuasca*.[18] He also had the opportunity to drink a tea produced from *ayahuasca* when carrying out research on the Conibo, another Upper Amazon Basin people, and this led him to appreciate the role of hallucinogenic experiences in the formation of indigenous belief systems. Although his studies with Upper Amazon shamans included the ingestion of indigenous hallucinogens, he subsequently learned non-hallucinogenic techniques of shamanism from North American Indian traditional healers.

Direct perception of the indigenously defined spirit world weakened his commitment to the conventional approaches of anthropology that emphasized symbolic interpretation. His participation in the visionary experiences of his informants reduced the distance between himself as an observer and the exotic lifeworld that he had temporarily entered. He began to understand perceptual experience as prior to ideology, and possibly the independent role of hallucinogens in the formation of cultural worldviews. From this viewpoint, shamanism was not a symbolic construction but a consequence of extraordinary perceptual experiences induced through a variety of methods, including hallucinogens.

While teaching at the New School for Social Research in New York City, Harner became increasingly involved in relating shamanic experiences to the concerns of everyday life in late capitalist American society. As a result he began to identify himself more with the personal practice of shamanism than with conventional anthropology. For him, the practical value and application of shamanic knowledge superseded the anthropological concerns of symbol and social structure. In 1980 he published a manual of shamanic practice.[19] Subsequently, in 1985, he established the Foundation for Shamanic Studies (FSS) to promote the revival and teaching of practical shamanism.[20] Among the shamanic techniques that Harner teaches are drumming, chanting, dancing, controlled visualization in the waking state, and awareness of dreams.

Harner's shamanism, promoted through the FSS as training programmes, is concerned with health in its broadest sense. As he describes it, shamanism employs ecstatic trances that make possible journeys to the invisible lower and upper worlds, populated by a great variety of spirit beings, for the purpose of attaining personal power. This power is intended to maintain an individual's well-being and to cure illnesses. He trains his students to practise non-hallucinogenic techniques to enter the shamanic state of consciousness in order to acquire personal power to benefit themselves, their patients, families, communities and the planet Earth. Unlike the way of the solitary sorcerer taught by Don Juan and Carlos Castaneda, Harner's training in healing shamanism is motivated by strong social concern.

The Foundation's mission to preserve indigenous shamanic knowledge is extended to its application for solving problems of contemporary society. Assistance is provided to native peoples throughout the world in recovering their lost or endangered traditional knowledge. The Foundation has created the title 'Living Treasure' to be awarded to gifted native shamans, along with a stipend, so that they will have adequate resources to transmit their knowledge. International projects carried out by the Foundation include the sending of a team to help the missionized Inuits of northern Canada in the rediscovery of their well-developed shamanic traditions. A Soviet–American shamanism programme was also started, and the Foundation was awarded a contract with the Russian Ministry of Health to implement shamanic healing methods in treating addictive and psychiatric problems.

The worldwide training programmes offered by the Foundation are consistent with its mission of knowledge preservation and healing. Core shamanism or universal methods of shamanism comprise the main content of the training programmes. Basic training in core shamanism covers the shamanic journey, power and healing. More advanced training is offered to students seeking in-depth knowledge of shamanic extraction healing, divination, nature spirits and the dying process. In addition, the Foundation conducts short courses on soul retrieval and special training in the Harner Method of Shamanic Counselling, which employs shamanic divination techniques and technological innovations. Information provided on the Foundation's website shows that its workshops and seminars are attended annually by at least 5000 people, including the participation of tribal peoples. The Foundation is also developing an archive of cross-cultural accounts of shamanic experiences, known as the Mapping of Non-ordinary Reality Project. The findings from this project are fed into the content of the training programmes.

All these activities of the FSS suggest that the recovery of shamanic knowledge by academics is no longer confined to the ivory tower, but systematized for solving problems in the wider society. Although Harner was trained in the anthropological technique of empathetic detachment, he went beyond this to embrace the shamanic practices of the peoples he studied. For him, shamanism was no longer an object of study cordoned off from the common-sense reality of Western bourgeois society. Rather, shamanism was treated as a practical reality continuous with the waking consciousness of everyday life. The retrieval and application of shamanic knowledge in contemporary society suggests that Harner and his associates make no special distinction between anthropology as an objective realm of knowledge concerning the lifeworlds of indigenous peoples and as a pragmatic system of applying indigenous knowledge. This development in the anthropology of shamanism implies a breakdown in the symbolic representation of shamanic knowledge. For Harner, the symbolic meanings attributed by anthropologists to shamanism lack efficacy unless they are transformed into precise instructions for the performance of healing and for movement in the spirit world.

In contemporary societies that are intensively influenced by sign culture, access to shamanism as a universal form of healing power rather than an exercise in symbolic interpretations widens the scope for market-oriented activities that promote the holistic treatment of mental and physical health. By disconnecting shamanic practices from the symbolic analyses of academic anthropology, Harner has succeeded in embedding those practices in a pragmatic system of signs that emphasizes the immediacy of the healing experience. The cultivation of this experience in workshops and seminars on shamanism enhances possibilities for direct contact with charisma, which forms the basis of a non-representational approach to the condition of generalized ecstasy. Thus, the recovery and application of shamanic knowledge in the contemporary world contribute to a post-Enlightenment understanding of charisma as a power of ecstasy and healing that is not always exclusive to virtuosos but immanent in our daily lives.

The Way of Dzogchen

The careers of Castaneda and Harner exemplify the transformation of disenchanted academics into re-enchanted shamans who attempt to disseminate their experiences and teachings to redefine, for the educated public, the meaning of non-ordinary realities. Unlike Castaneda and Harner, Namkhai Norbu is not from a disenchanted academic background. His cultural and religious expertise was obtained in traditional Tibetan monasteries and from personalized tutelage with several masters of shamanic knowledge.[21]

Although Namkhai Norbu is not a shaman in the traditional sense of the word, his training in esoteric Buddhism with links to the Bön religion of ancient Tibet distinguishes him from the secular scholars of Tibetan history and culture. His position in a Western university is, therefore, unique because he is able to preserve and transmit shamanic knowledge from the citadels of higher learning in secular society. However, he is not the only Tibetan with religious and shamanic training to be ensconced in a Western university. Other highly regarded Tibetan lamas have taken up academic positions in the West following the Chinese takeover of Tibet in 1959.[22] In providing institutional space for traditional Tibetan teachers, Western universities have played a significant role in the process of re-enchantment.

The university has been a valuable resource for Namkhai Norbu to introduce the educated middle classes to a monistic worldview and shamanic practices. In 1960 the renowned Tibetologist, Giuseppe Tucci, invited him to teach in Italy. In 1964 he became a professor of Mongolian and Tibetan language and culture at the Instituto Orientale, University of Naples. In addition to his academic activities, he teaches Dzogchen around the world. Dzogchen represents the highest teachings to have been produced from the close connections between the Nyingma sect of Tibetan Buddhism and the ancient Bön religion. According to Samuel, its origins are obscure but probably reflect the interaction of Indian and Chinese shamanic elements in eighth-century Tibet.[23] In essence, Dzogchen is a 'formless and nonconceptual system of meditation, conceived of ... as the final stage of Tantric practice ...'.[24]

Eminent Tibetan lamas recognized the young Namkhai Norbu as the mind incarnation of Pema Karpo, a great religious master who contributed to the founding of Bhutan and its line of spiritual and temporal rulers. He was also recognized as the reincarnation of Adzam Drugpa, a great Dzogchen master, who, in turn, was reputed to be a reincarnation of Pema Karpo. Namkhai Norbu is therefore, regarded as the reunification of the two separate incarnations of Pema Karpo and Adzam Drugpa.[25] Although he underwent intensive monastic training in eastern Tibet, he did not become a monk and remains a lay practitioner, leading an outwardly ordinary life as a family man and academic in Italy, while teaching Dzogchen as a practice of everyday life. Because he studied with both Bön and Buddhist teachers, he can be described as a Dzogchen practitioner in the Rimed tradition.[26]

According to Namkhai Norbu, Dzogchen is a way of perceiving and being, which frees the practitioner from distorted cognition and emotions.[27] Anyone can practise Dzogchen and experience primordial awareness that has been temporarily obscured by dualistic perception. By engaging in the practice of Dzogchen, the practitioner comes to experience non-dual awareness of phenomena, at first occasionally and then continuously. This uninterrupted awareness leads Dzogchen practitioners to personally experience the illusory nature of the self. They become cognizant of all phenomena, including the self, as flows of energy to be simply observed without judgement.

Although Dzogchen is an anti-foundational teaching that affirms no ontology beyond the flow and continuation of energy, its practice rests on the foundation of the guru–disciple relationship. For Namkhai Norbu, the relationship with his principal guru began with a dream[28] about someone called Changchub Dorje and the house and village where he resided, in which he sensed that he had met his principal master. He used this information in a search that led to an ordinary-looking old man and a milieu that corresponded exactly to the dream. Having confirmed his dream link to Changchub Dorje, he was accepted as a student.

Although Namkhai Norbu had already studied in monastic colleges with many teachers, only Changchub Dorje imparted to him the Dzogchen experience of non-duality. Without relying on any formal rituals, Changchub Dorje was able to transmit directly to Namkhai Norbu the experience of non-duality. This direct transmission taught him the precarious nature of conventional concepts and the effective use of ordinary circumstances as occasions for contemplating non-duality.[29] Even after he fled from the political upheavals in Tibet and found refuge abroad, his guru manifested to him in dreams and gave him advanced teachings. These experiences revealed the unhindered flow of charisma through the guru–disciple relationship, without regard to time and space. Namkhai Norbu himself sometimes communicates with his students by appearing in their dreams.[30] He involves his students actively in dream-transmitted teachings by enlisting their help in recording the instructions and texts that he has received. New insights and practices received in dreams reinforce the charismatic relationship between guru and disciples.

Dream yoga, which Namkhai Norbu teaches as a secondary practice, links Dzogchen to shamanism. It comprises techniques for developing the illusory body, which is the dream image of the physical body so that someone who has mastered dream yoga is able to use the illusory body to accomplish what is conventionally regarded as extraordinary. Protection and healing through dream yoga are salient everyday concerns that involve Dzogchen practitioners.

One of Namkhai Norbu's students, Michael Katz, gave an account of shamanic healing carried out in the dream state for a female student who had become seriously ill.[31] While attending a seminar in Washington DC, Katz dreamed of being informed by his guru that the ailing student had been treated and was recovering. The following day, Katz found that her recovery was underway and that his guru was aware of the dream conversation. In another anecdote, Namkhai Norbu related a dream episode in which he delivered a message from a deity to one of his uncles.[32] He was aware that it was a dream throughout the entire event. Upon waking, he delivered the message to his uncle who remarked that he had been expecting it. His uncle proceeded to follow the instructions in the message, which led him to discover a *terma* or treasure teaching.[33]

The mastery of dreams is, therefore, integral to the Dzogchen path of attaining primordial awareness as taught by Namkhai Norbu. As a classic shamanic technique, dreaming provides the practitioner with more than just an assessment of symbolic action in an altered state of consciousness. Shamanic dreaming transforms dream symbols into signposts of new experiences that are not distinguished from the perceptions of everyday life. Indeed, the practice of dream yoga for healing, teaching and other purposes is not inconsistent with Namkhai Norbu's emphasis on the spontaneous, non-dual nature of reality and he does, in fact, refer to dreams of clarity that close the gap between dreaming and waking consciousness.[34] By maintaining the continuity between dreaming and waking, the structures of disenchantment are called into question. The separation of phenomena and states of consciousness, so characteristic of the disenchanted world, becomes a hindrance to academic shamans who endeavour to sensitize the educated public to the undifferentiated nature of consciousness.

Symbolism in Asian Shamanism

The reinvention of shamanism in the West through the New Age movement, based on bestselling books and seminars that provide practical instruction for a mass market of seekers, converges with the reinvigoration of shamanism rooted in Asian traditions. These developments are the outcome of activity on the part of the Asian and Western middle classes who unhesitatingly employ the pragmatism of modernity to promote an archaic practice in an increasingly rationalized world. While the disenchanted Western bourgeoisie have been rediscovering shamanism, shamanism in Asia has never been expunged from the cultural and religious landscape. Despite the influence of the world religions, modern science and commerce on the Asian middle classes, their connections to indigenous shamanic traditions have not been entirely severed.

The Asian bourgeoisie employ shamanism to satisfy practical needs, including the construction of collective identities. Unlike New Age shamanism, which has emerged within the culture of signs, Asian shamanism remains firmly attached to symbolic structures of meaning, being embedded within a traditional cosmology that is a source of symbols of collective identities. The pragmatism of the Asian bourgeoisie, which motivates their involvement in shamanism, tends to be oriented more towards the symbol than the sign. Participation in Asian shamanism entails emotional and cognitive commitments that, for the most part, do not feature in New Age shamanism.

Unlike New Age shamans, Asian shamans tend to manipulate symbolic structures to mediate the tensions between tradition and modernity. These tensions originated from the intrusion of Western capital and knowledge into the enchanted cosmos of Asian societies. Although many Asian societies attempted to resist Western domination, the pragmatics of sheer survival motivated Asian adaptation to, and mastery of, modernity. However, Asian efforts to come to terms with modernity did not result in the disenchantment of the magical cosmos because of the way Asians adapted to modernity. The coexistence of an enchanted world with modern capitalism gave rise to alternative forms of meaning in the Asian magical cosmos. From the modern perspective, beliefs and actions oriented towards enchanted worlds were denigrated as superstition. What had been unreflective participation in an undifferentiated cosmos became increasingly self-conscious, thus generating tensions within the traditional perspective itself. It was these tensions that motivated urban middle-class Asians to seek a *rapprochement* between their traditional beliefs and the world of technology and industry in which they earned their living. To reach this understanding required a position of cultivated ambivalence straddling the opposing realms of science and magic. Thus, Asians steeped in the magical cosmos may attend schools emphasizing science-based curriculum or work for multinational employers and in occupations dependent on Western forms of organization and technology.

It is in the juxtaposition of enchanted and disenchanted worlds that we find the emergence of a shamanism that is highly self-conscious about the use of concepts and practices condemned by the educated elite as primitive. This shamanism can best be described as a modern form of magical practice facilitating the development of reflexive discourses that not only provide a rationalized means for bridging the realms of science and magic, but also the groundwork for establishing organized movements emphasizing individual and collective identities.

The eclectic approach of modern shamans makes possible the infusion of new ingredients in the construction of reflexive discourses. Symbols and signs alike can be readily accepted as elements to be reworked within the framework of traditional cosmologies. The magical cosmos within which modern Asian shamans create their discourses is characterized by flexible boundaries. The fluidity of this cosmos brings the symbol and sign into juxtaposition with little or no tension.

The work of modern Asian shamanic movements involves the fashioning of reflexive discourses from indigenous traditions and their dissemination by technical means. As the scope of discursive shamanism is extended beyond the local level through print, broadcasting and electronic communication, symbols are gradually detached from traditional structures of meaning to enter spiritual markets. The symbols constituting shamanic discourses are transformed into signs as they become commodified images. A selection of modern Asian shamanic movements described below suggests a shift from traditional symbolic transactions to a condition of overlapping regimes of signification.

Shamanic Textualism

The role of symbols in renewing collective identities can be observed in the production of shamanic texts in Chinese spirit-writing cults. These cults in Taiwan produce shamanic texts known as morality books (*shan shu*), which they seek to distribute widely for the spiritual edification of the public. Jordan and Overmeyer provide a detailed account of such groups, and the role of middle-class individuals in the production of shamanic texts.[35] This variety of shamanism features an entranced planchette wielder who makes contact with divinities and spirits from the traditional Chinese pantheon and writes their messages in sand. The messages are subsequently recorded and compiled by a scribe. Public donations finance the printing and distribution of the resulting texts.

The Sheng Xian Tang, a temple in Taichung, Taiwan, has a resident planchette wielder whose spirit writings over a 22-month period culminated in a shamanic text narrating his travels to the lower realms of the traditional Chinese cosmos. The text, first published in Chinese in Taiwan, reached a Chinese religious group in Malaysia that sponsored further Chinese editions as well as the translation and publication of the text in English. The sponsors sought to make this text available to English-educated Malaysian Chinese who are illiterate in Chinese.[36]

Published in English under the title *Journeys to the Underworld*,[37] the text begins with an edict from the Jade Emperor (the supreme god of the highest heaven in the Chinese pantheon) to commission the Sheng Xian Tang's shaman to make a series of visits to the 10 tribunals of the Chinese underworld that are to be recorded and published for the benefit of modern people who no longer take the tenets of Chinese cosmology seriously. These narratives of shamanic journeys are intended to impress the secular world with the concrete reality of sin, virtue, reward and punishment. This form of shamanism upholds Confucian family-based morality and popular cosmological beliefs by reinforcing traditional Chinese symbols. The text includes diagrams of the sacred cosmos, drawings of the tribunals of hell and dialogues with deities.

The Jade Emperor's edict defined the commissioned text as a record of teachings to be distributed free of charge to the public. The circulation of the text as a gift was made possible by donations of labour, skill, equipment and money from individuals within a wide network of Chinese religious groups. The voluntary nature of this event meant that shamanic labour and the receipt of moral teachings were not defined as commodities. Rather, the experiences of the shaman and the moral concerns of the laypeople were bonded through symbolic exchange focusing on the attainment of merit. A statement at the beginning of the text announced that combined divine and human efforts in the production of the text generated merit as a positive moral force. Thus, a moral community was sustained by the voluntary production and distribution of a text, the value of which was not calculable as a commodity but as merit stemming from symbolic exchange. This exchange could be seen as a form of moral reciprocity between humans and deities for creating the merit necessary for salvation in the heavenly realms of the magical cosmos. The shaman mediated this exchange through his ability to travel to other realms of existence.

Symbolic exchange in shamanic spirit-writing is also associated with discourses of collective identity. Such activities were observed in a modern Chinese spirit-writing movement in Kuala Lumpur, Malaysia. This movement, the Goddess of Mercy Devotional Society, was founded by Master Chan.[38] After establishing communication with the Goddess of Mercy (*Guanyin*) through the mediation of several popular Chinese deities, Master Chan was specially commissioned to reach out to English-speaking, middle-class Chinese alienated from their traditional beliefs. Through spirit-writing in English, Master Chan has produced a shamanic text relating his experiences and communications with the Goddess of Mercy and other deities from the Chinese pantheon.

Many of the Goddess of Mercy's messages concerned the relevance of traditional Chinese cosmology and morality to modern people. These messages have been recorded over the course of more than 20 years in a stack of ledger books stored in the shrine hall that Master Chan maintained for devotion and service to the Goddess of Mercy. Although these ledger books were not published at the time of our research, they nevertheless formed an extended shamanic text narrating Master Chan's entrance into the traditional cosmos, his receipt of special blessings and spiritual power from *Guanyin*, and his responsibilities to heal and teach all who approached him.

This shamanic text was available to all devotees who were interested in Master Chan's teachings. By reading this text, English-speaking Chinese were given the opportunity to rediscover their traditional religious roots and reconstruct their identities based on an understanding of *Guanyin*'s messages. In this sense, the text symbolized a close exchange between a modern shaman-teacher with direct access to *Guanyin*'s power and some Chinese who sought merit within the realm of traditional Chinese deities.

Like the Chinese, Tibetans also have records of shamans who travel to other realms and return to the ordinary world to give accounts of their experiences. Known in Tibetan as *delogs*, these shamans undertake perilous journeys to benefit others by verifying Buddhist cosmology and its moral relevance. Shamanic texts are produced from a *delog*'s visionary experiences. Although *delog* texts resemble the *shan shu* of Chinese spirit-writing cults, this form of Tibetan shamanism is far more dramatic. Unlike the planchette wielding Chinese shaman, a *delog* enters a death-like, comatose state that may last several days, or even a week. While in this state, a *delog*'s consciousness is said to travel freely through the upper and lower realms of the cosmos, encountering various non-physical beings. Because such journeys are fraught with hazards, it is not unusual for shamanic deaths to occur.

Delogs who return to embodied reality with beneficial teachings for their communities are considered to have attained a remarkable spiritual accomplishment. One such *delog* was the revered female shaman, Dawa Drolma. In 1987 her son, Chagdud Tulku, a lama who fled Tibet in 1959 and subsequently found refuge in the United States, retrieved from his sister the only existing copy of their mother's *delog* experiences. When he brought the text to the United States, his students helped him to translate it into English for publication.[39]

According to the text, in 1924, when Dawa Drolma was 16 years old, she received instructions from the wisdom goddess, White Tara, to prepare for a journey to other realms. She remained comatose for five full days when she embarked on that journey. Upon her return, she narrated her experiences to a scribe who recorded them in longhand. The resulting text, describing her visions of deities in their abodes and the messages she received to be communicated to human beings, became the basis of spiritual teachings for the Tibetan Buddhist laity.

Although Dawa Drolma's account of her spiritual journey was textualized for religious purposes in Tibet, her narrative has now been published and distributed in the West. This development suggests that the circle of symbolic exchange has widened to possibly include readers who may not be Buddhists but seek re-enchantment in their lives. Unlike the Chinese shamanic texts described earlier, the publication in the West of Dawa Drolma's *delog* experiences signals a revival of shamanic knowledge that extends beyond a closed or limited circle of devotees. In the New Age, such texts may come to be treated as part and parcel of a growing public fascination with personal experiences of a shamanic nature that defy the routines of everyday life.

Symbols of Protest

Modern shamanism in Korea has emerged orally in the form of countercultural performances.[40] Students, academics and other Korean intellectuals have adopted shamanic elements of peasant culture to create public performances that invoke and exorcise spirits for the purposes of political protest. Folk music, dance, drama and shamanic rituals are synthesized into oral texts that oppose the official culture of the patriarchal state. Shamanic rituals provide radical intellectuals with symbolic resources to fashion alternative political discourses that define identity, culture, justice, democracy and human rights on a basis claimed to be authentically nationalist. Korean labour struggles have also adopted shamanic performances as a mode of public protest.

This form of shamanic activity has been a regular feature of Korean public protest since the early 1970s when it was used in reaction to the government-initiated modernization programmes at the end of the 1960s. Modernization under the auspices of the authoritarian state widened the gap between the ruling elite, perceived as corrupt, and the masses. For many ordinary Koreans, shamanism remains part of everyday life, and transactions with deities take place in the mundane language of the marketplace. These transactions are based on egalitarian relationships between humans and deities, thus serving as an alternative model of power to the authoritarian state. Shamanism does not posit the hegemony of a supreme being, and submission to a centralized spiritual power is not a feature of shamanic ideology. Rather, it is based on the belief that human beings can beneficially communicate with a multiplicity of spiritual powers. This indigenous worldview complements Korean struggles for a democratic and just social order.

Symbols of Purification

Flourishing in charismatic new religions, Japanese shamanism attracts middle-class participation in the symbolic work of overcoming illnesses and misfortunes, assimilating industrial society into animistic folk traditions, and reconstructing cultural identity as Japan rapidly internationalizes.

Mahikari and Agonshu are among the bumper crop of new religions originating from shamanic experiences in postwar Japan. The founders of these two new religions transcended personal adversity by visiting the spirit world and returning to everyday life with a message of salvation for humanity. The message fundamentally concerned practical methods of bringing spiritual power into solving problems of everyday life. Purification and exorcism, known as *okiyome*, is the centrepiece of the Mahikari path to salvation.[41] Agonshu, by contrast, promotes mass participation in dramatic fire rituals to bring about salvation for both the living and departed.[42]

Like most other Japanese new religions, Mahikari and Agonshu draw upon folk traditions in diagnosing and managing the human condition. According to popular religious beliefs, suffering is caused by the influences of unhappy departed spirits. In particular, the spirits of one's ancestors exert a decisive influence on the activities of this world. Mahikari teaches that most illnesses and misfortunes are the result of spirit possession and that unhappy ancestors can wreak the greatest havoc on an individual's life. Purification and exorcism of these spirits can be accomplished through *okiyome* – the method of directing spiritual energy from the palms of upraised hands towards the possessed person. *Okiyome* treatment transforms evil spirits into benevolent guardians or drives them back to the spirit world and, when it is performed effectively, the individual's problems are eliminated.

Agonshu offers a similar diagnosis but seeks to pacify angry, restless spirits through *goma* – fire rituals – whereby petitions written on *gomagi* (wooden tablets) are offered on a pyre. The burning bundles of *gomagi* purify and liberate the spirits that afflict the petitioners. The spirits are then transformed into buddhas who will protect and bless their descendents.

Like other Japanese new religions, Mahikari and Agonshu make use of the mass media to disseminate their teachings. Mahikari videotapes demonstrations of *okiyome* and possessed persons' responses to this treatment. Agonshu produces films, videotapes and television footage of its extravagant fire rituals. For example, Agonshu's annual fire ritual held in Kyoto is televised live throughout Japan.[43]

The cases of Mahikari and Agonshu demonstrate how elements of shamanism in postwar Japan have been transformed into mass movements that employ modern technology to propagate traditional cosmology in a predominantly urban, middle-class population. This traditional cosmology provides the symbolic ingredients for reconstructing Japanese identity. Ironically, symbolic reconstruction of Japanese identity is occurring within a context of televised imagery that opens the way to the proliferation of signs. In other words, modern Japanese shamanism draws on traditional symbols for promoting purification in mass movements that are being consolidated in a postmodern culture of signs. Mahikari and Agonshu represent shamanically inspired new religions that stand at the borders between symbolic cosmology and the theatre of signs. They signify the postmodern transformation of shamanism into a form of enchanted spectacle for renewing personal and collective identities.

Falungong: Between Symbol and Sign

Falungong is a new cultural movement that emerged in China in the early 1990s. Because it revitalizes traditional Chinese symbols, it is perceived by the Chinese communist government as a challenge to its authority and has been banned in China. Nevertheless, it has found many adherents around the world, many of whom are urban, middle-class individuals attracted to the movement for its spiritual teachings and *qigong* practices.[44]

Its leader, Li Hongzhi, a former government employee, claims to possess the ability to help people by adjusting their internal energies to open them to higher levels of consciousness.[45] Li was active in the *qigong* movement that emerged in post-Mao China. During that period, exponents of *qigong* succeeded in developing an international market for traditional Chinese health practices.[46] Li combined *qigong* practices with his interpretation of Mahayana Buddhism to found Falungong.

Central to Li's teachings is the Taoist view of the universe as existing in a dynamic balance of yin and yang forces.[47] These teachings guide practitioners in attaining a balanced flow of *qi* (energy) within the body. He emphasizes morality based on truth, goodness and forbearance as integral to *qigong* practices. In his view, moral transgressions produce bad karma which results in energy blockages and imbalances. Practitioners can restore and maintain their health by following his teachings on *qi* and moral practices. His teachings have been compiled into multiple volumes, resembling the morality books produced by Chinese shamans described earlier. Available in Chinese, English and other languages, his teachings are disseminated globally from Falungong websites on the Internet.[48]

Falungong shares a background of moral teachings, eclectic symbols and shamanic empowerment with many popular heterodox movements in Chinese history.[49] Nevertheless, there are several important differences. Unlike many popular movements that were supported by large peasant followings, Falungong is urban-based and attracts literate people familiar with the latest technology. Recruitment is not limited to Chinese followers; there are many non-Chinese Falungong members in the West.[50] It can be considered a 'virtual movement' rather than an institution because it extensively employs electronic communications on the Internet to build a global movement.[51]

Falungong breathed new life into traditional Chinese symbols by offering an ideological alternative to communism in China. The growing number of Falungong followers throughout Chinese society, especially within the state apparatuses, aroused concern. By the mid-1990s, the Chinese authorities viewed Falungong with apprehension, fearing that its activities were possibly spearheading the development of civil society. The movement's ability to mobilize large-scale assemblies, and its claims to a higher truth superseding communist ideology, was perceived to threaten the legitimacy of the Chinese state. Consequently, the Chinese government banned Falungong in 1999 and conducted an intensive campaign to discredit the movement. Li went into exile in the United States and it was reported many of his followers in China were detained. Yet, as a 'virtual movement', Falungong is able to continue its activities and attract followers from all over the world, claiming, since 1999, to have 100 million followers. The movement is active in at least 30 countries and maintains more than 60 websites in the United States alone.[52]

Like many new shamanic movements in Asia, Falungong systematized symbolic elements of folk religion in ways that appealed to middle-class seekers. At the same time, the movement also made use of scientific symbols approved by the Chinese authorities. For instance, *qigong* practices were defined by the Chinese state as an indigenous contribution to modern health-care services. Symbolic syncretism in Falungong enables it to attract followers from all walks of life. The combination of folk and scientific symbols, together with shamanic healing, not only makes Falungong acceptable to many people in Chinese society, but also presents it as compatible with the New Age movement in the West. New Age seekers who turn to Asian religions for spiritual inspiration may find Falungong appealing because it emphasizes internal development and healing within the framework of traditional symbols and scientific knowledge.

Falungong's conflict with the Chinese government has turned it into a political symbol against state authoritarianism. Followers who claim that there is nothing sinister about the movement's beliefs and practices interpret the crackdown by the Chinese authorities as a violation of human rights. The Chinese authorities, on the other hand, perceive Falungong as an 'evil cult' that brainwashes followers and harbours the intention to overthrow the government.[53] A war of symbols between the movement and the Chinese government has now entered cyberspace. Operating as a 'virtual movement', Falungong is able to use its websites to disseminate information on spiritual and political activities. The Chinese authorities have set up anti-Falungong websites to counter the movement's electronic communications.

This unprecedented development in the history of Chinese religions suggests that symbolic meanings concerning health and spiritual transcendence can be transformed into the images of global sign culture, that can circulate unhindered in cyberspace and are available to Internet users. Electronic communication technologies extract Falungong from local cultural space, turning it into a conglomeration of signs occupying impersonal space beyond state control. The presence of Falungong on the Internet implies that state control of heterodox religious activities is limited by the power of sign culture. The movement's literature is available on the main websites and can be downloaded without payment. As signs that circulate freely, the movement's literature has become part of a wider network of consumer spiritualism catering to middle-class seekers of alternative beliefs and practices.

The coincidence of religious innovation and political protest in Falungong presages the simultaneity of symbol and sign in global culture. Symbols continue to operate as vehicles of cultural and political meaning in specific contexts of social change, but they lose all exclusive meaning by entering cyberspace. As signs, they are disconnected from specific structures of meaning to become free-floating objects for consumption.

Shamanic movements that work on these two levels present a new phenomenon that supersedes the older heterodox religious movements in Chinese history.

Asian Shamanism Meets the New Age

The New Age has made it possible for shamanism to be revived as part of the process of re-enchantment in the West. It has also opened the way for Asian shamanic traditions to be reinvented on a wider scale for thaumaturgical, political and various cultural reasons. The common denominator that connects New Age shamanism to Asian shamanic traditions is technology which has contributed significantly both to the development of modern Asian shamanism and the re-enchantment of Western societies by objectifying ecstatic experiences. At present, the main technical means used to accomplish this include printing, audio- and videotapes, films, telecasts, online electronic communication and mass marketing. The systematization of ecstatic experiences through these means has propelled shamanism beyond the personalized encounters that generally characterize the relationship between guru and disciple.

In the New Age, shamanism has come to occupy wider public spaces and to be democratically available to all interested seekers. For example, shamanic dreaming has become an option for any individual when the means of consciously entering the dream state are broadly disseminated. Similarly, new religions with shamanic characteristics may provide individual followers with the opportunity to develop self-healing abilities. Thus, the meaning of shamanism in Asia and the West is converging with rapid technological developments to produce new patterns of mass participation that accentuate the immanence of charisma.

Aided by technology, these new forms of shamanism find their most vibrant expression in middle-class society. In Asia, middle-class seekers objectify shamanism by using their technical skills to restore and enhance the meaning of traditional cosmologies for consolidating personal and collective identities. But, unlike their New Age counterparts in the West, Asian shamanic resurgence is still rooted in symbolic structures that maintain values of exchange and reciprocity. However, this symbolic pattern may be changing for two reasons. First, the eclecticism of the New Age movement predisposes it towards an exploration and adaptation of Asian shamanic traditions for the purposes of self-healing and enhancing human potential. Because the New Age movement is immersed in the culture of signs, any adaptation of Asian shamanism quickly becomes commoditized as an item of consumption in authenticating personal experiences. Second, the process of globalization may facilitate the exportation of New Age shamanism to Asian societies with expanding middle classes whose members traverse symbolic and sign cultures. By engaging in New Age shamanism, members of the Asian bourgeoisie may gradually come to take on the characteristics associated with the emergence of sign culture.

In the New Age, shamanism sheds its traditional garb to take on new characteristics that are compatible with technological innovations. As shamanism penetrates the belief system and lifestyle of the middle classes, new forms of spiritual consciousness develop to mix tradition and technology in unexpected ways. The tradition of shamanic dreaming is one area of healing that is being transformed into a dynamic practice of consciousness expansion, as we will see in the next chapter.

Notes

1 For a broad survey of shamanic practices around the world, see Mircea Eliade (1964), *Shamanism: Archaic Techniques of Ecstasy*, Princeton, NJ: Princeton University Press.

2 For example, see Vittorio Lanternari (1963), *The Religions of the Oppressed*, New York: Alfred Knopf; Bryan R. Wilson (1973), *Magic and the Millennium*, New York: Harper and Row.

3 See Paul Heelas (1996), *The New Age Movement*, Oxford: Blackwell, pp.29, 47, 53, 89.

4 See Robert S. Ellwood, Jr (1973), *Religious and Spiritual Groups in Modern America*, Englewood Cliffs, NJ: Prentice Hall, pp.11–18.

5 See Barbara G. Myerhoff (1974), *Peyote Hunt*, Ithaca, NY: Cornell University Press; Marlene Dobkin de Rios (1972), *Visionary Vine*, San Francisco: Chandler.

6 Castaneda published 12 books on his experiences with Don Juan Matus and shamanic realities. See Carlos Castaneda (1968), *The Teachings of Don Juan*, New York: Ballantine Books; idem (1971), *A Separate Reality*, New York: Simon and Schuster; idem (1972), *Journey to Ixtlan*, New York: Simon and Schuster; idem (1974), *Tales of Power*, New York: Simon and Schuster; idem (1977), *The Second Ring of Power*, New York: Simon and Schuster; idem (1981), *The Eagle's Gift*, New York: Simon and Schuster; idem (1984), *The Fire From Within*, New York: Simon and Schuster; idem (1991), *The Power of Silence*, New York: Pocket Books; idem (1994), *The Art of Dreaming*. New York: Harper; idem (1998), *The Wheel of Time*, Los Angeles: Eidolona Press; idem (1998), *Magical Passes*, New York: HarperCollins; idem (1998), *The Active Side of Infinity*, New York: HarperCollins.

7 Sceptical and favourable reviews of Castaneda's works have been compiled by Daniel Noel (ed.) (1976), *Seeing Castaneda: Reactions to the 'Don Juan' Writings of Carlos Castaneda*, New York: Putnam. For a more critical assessment of Castaneda's works, see Richard De Mille (1976), *Castaneda's Journey: The Power and the Allegory*, Santa Barbara, CA: Capra Press; and idem (1980), *The Don Juan Papers*. Santa Barbara, CA: Ross Erickson.

8 From his third book, *Journey to Ixtlan*, to the last, *The Active Side of Infinity*, the art of dreaming superseded altered states of consciousness arising from hallucinogens.

9 Castaneda, *Journey to Ixtlan*, *op.cit.*, pp.97–100.

10 As reported in Castaneda, *The Second Ring of Power* and *The Eagle's Gift*, *op.cit.*

11 See Castaneda, *The Eagle's Gift*, *op.cit.*

12 For information on Castaneda's association with these organizations, see his interview with Daniel Trujillo Rivas, 'Navigating into the Unknown: An Interview with Carlos Castaneda' for the magazine *Uno Mismo*, Chile and Argentina, February 1997. Also accessible on the website <www.castaneda.com>.

13 This is explained in the statement, 'What is Tensegrity?' available on the website <www.castaneda.com>. See also Carlos Castaneda (1998), 'Magical Passes', *Yoga Journal*, January, available on the website <www.nagual.net>.
14 Castaneda asserted that he made the magical passes available to the public because of the reappearance of Carol Tiggs, a Don Juan disciple, in 1985 from an alternative reality. See Mick Brown (1998), 'Shaman or Sham?', *Electronic Telegraph*, 1 August, Issue 1163. Available on the website <www.nagual.net>.
15 See Elizabeth Kaye McCall (1996), 'Journeys with Carlos Castaneda's Tensegrity', *Sedona Journal*, October; M.V. Moorhead (1996), 'Shaman U', *Phoenix New Times*. Available on the website <www.nagual.net>.
16 See 'Purpose of Tensegrity Seminars', available on the website <www.castaneda.com>.
17 See Brown, 'Shaman or Sham?', *op. cit.*
18 Michael J. Harner (1973), 'The Sound of Rushing Water', in M.J. Harner (ed.), *Hallucinogens and Shamanism*, New York: Oxford University Press, pp.15–27.
19 Michael Harner (1980), *The Way of the Shaman*, New York: Harper and Row.
20 All information on the FSS was accessed from the website <www.shamanism.org>.
21 For some information on Namkhai Norbu's background, see Stephen Batchelor (1994), *The Awakening of the West: The Encounter of Buddhism and Western Culture*, Berkeley, CA: Parallax, pp.76–7.
22 For example, Jigme Norbu at Indiana University, Geshe Sopa Rinpoche at the University of Wisconsin, and Dagpo Rinpoche at the Sorbonne in Paris.
23 Geoffrey Samuel, *Civilized Shamans: Buddhism in Tibetan Societies*. Washington, DC: Smithsonian Institution 1993, p.463.
24 Ibid., p.464.
25 Chögyal Namkhai Norbu (1996), *Dzogchen: The Self-Perfected State*, Ithaca, NY: Snow Lion, pp.11–12.
26 Rimed is a non-sectarian movement that became influential in eastern Tibet among monks and laymen from the nineteenth century onwards. See Samuel, *Civilized Shamans*, *op.cit.*, pp.525–53.
27 Namkhai Norbu (1993), *The Crystal and the Way of Light*, New York: Arkana, pp.11–15.
28 Ibid., pp.8–10.
29 Ibid., pp.15–20.
30 Namkhai Norbu (1992), *Dream Yoga and the Practice of Natural Light*, Ithaca, NY: Snow Lion, p.12.
31 Ibid.
32 Namkhai Norbu, *The Crystal and the Way of Light*, *op.cit.*, pp.51–2.
33 The Tibetan *terma* tradition of finding hidden teachings is closely associated with Padmasambhava, the yogi-shaman who introduced tantric Buddhism to Tibet in the second half of the eighth century CE.
34 Namkhai Norbu, *Dream Yoga and the Practice of Natural Light*, *op.cit.*, p.104.
35 David K. Jordan and Daniel L. Overmeyer (1986), *The Flying Phoenix: Aspects of Chinese Sectarianism in Taiwan*, Princeton, NJ: Princeton University Press.
36 Chinese comprise about 27 per cent of the population in Malaysia. The majority of them are Buddhists and Taoists. A substantial section of Malaysian Chinese was educated in English during the colonial period and after independence in 1957. They are illiterate in Chinese, although many of them speak Chinese dialects. The enchanted worldviews of many Chinese in Malaysia have not been eroded by modernization. See Raymond L.M. Lee and Susan E. Ackerman (1997), *Sacred Tensions: Modernity and Religious Transformation in Malaysia*, Columbia, SC: University of South Carolina Press.
37 *Journeys to the Underworld*, Kuala Lumpur: De Jiao Hong Yang She, 1987.
38 We have given pseudonyms to the society and its founder to protect their identities. Observations on the society were made by the second author between 1990 and 1995.

See Susan E. Ackerman (2001), 'Divine Contracts: Chinese New Religions and Shamanic Movements in Contemporary Malaysia', *Journal of Contemporary Religion*, 16(3), pp.293–311.

39 See Delog Dawa Drolma (1995), *Delog: Journey to Realms Beyond Death*, Junction City, CA: Padma Publishing.

40 The discussion here is based largely on materials from Kwang-Ok Kim (1994), 'Rituals of Resistance: The Manipulation of Shamanism in Contemporary Korea', in C. Keyes, L. Kendall and H. Hardacre (eds), *Asian Visions of Authority: Religion and the Modern States of East and Southeast Asia*, Honolulu, HI: University of Hawaii Press, pp.195–219.

41 See Winston Davis (1980), *Dojo: Magic and Exorcism in Modern Japan*, Stanford, CA: Stanford University Press.

42 See Ian Reader (1991), *Religion in Contemporary Japan*, London: Macmillan.

43 Ibid., pp. 208, 218–19.

44 *Qigong* is a Taoist-inspired slow-moving exercise performed for health and endurance. It is often combined with *Taijichuan* and other martial arts. The purpose of *qigong* exercise is balanced circulation of vital energy within the body. A *qigong* master is able to direct cosmic energy to enhance health and longevity, and instructs others in these techniques. *Qigong* is sometimes referred to as 'Chinese yoga' and is related to tantric practices involving the control and transformation of psychophysical energies.

45 See Li Hongzhi (2001), *Falun Gong*, Chapter 1. Available online at <www.falundafa.org>.

46 See David Ownby (2000), 'Falungong as a Cultural Revitalization Movement: An Historian Looks at Contemporary China', talk given at Rice University, 20 October. Available online at <www.ruf.edu/~tnchina/commentary/ownby1000.html>

47 Interaction of negative (yin) and positive (yang) energies is the source of all phenomena, according to Taoist philosophy. These energies are always in motion; thus, change and fluctuation are the inherent conditions of the cosmos.

48 The website is <www.falundafa.org/eng/index.en.htm>.

49 See Frederick Wakeman, Jr (1977), 'Rebellion and Revolution: The Study of Popular Movements in Chinese History', *Journal of Asian Studies*, 36(2), pp.1–37; Daniel L. Overmyer (1981), 'Alternatives: Popular Religious Sects in Chinese Society', *Modern China*, 7(2), pp.153–90.

50 See Jonathan Landreth (2001), 'Falun Gong Draws Americans', Reuters article in *The Sun* (Malaysia), 12 May.

51 As noted by Barend Ter Haar (2001), 'Falun Gong: Evaluation and Further References'. Available on-line at <www.let.leidenuniv.nl/bth/falun.htm>.

52 Patsy Rahn (2000), 'The Falun Gong: Beyond the Headlines', paper presented at the American Family Foundation's annual conference, 28 April. Available on-line at <www.let.leidenuniv.nl/bth/FalunRAHN.htm>

53 See Landreth, 'Falun Gong Draws Americans', *op. cit.*

Chapter 6

The New Religion of Dreaming

The original argonauts of the dream world were shamans. They lived and practised in premodern cultures that did not make exclusive distinctions between waking life and other realms of non-waking consciousness. In these cultures, shamanic dreaming was a power in itself because it was the gateway to unique experiences and special knowledge. Dreams played a vital role in the shaman's initiation and in his quest for healing powers. This was well documented by Mircea Eliade who pointed out that for shamans, '[i]t is in dreams that the pure sacred life is entered and direct relations with the gods, spirits, and ancestral souls are re-established'.[1] Shamanic dreaming was no mean feat for individuals who sought knowledge and power beyond the confines of waking life.

In many premodern and modernizing societies, shamanic dreaming formed the basis of traditional religions and new religious movements. Through dream experiences, interpreted as having special significance for spiritual accomplishments, shamans and gifted individuals were able to influence their followers to participate in religious movements that renewed the meaning of tradition or challenged the power of the state. Dreams were not dismissed as frivolous expressions of the sleeping mind, but accepted as paths to creative knowledge for changing a person's lifestyle and the conditions of social existence.

At the beginning of the twenty-first century, we witness a growing interest in the dynamics of dream consciousness. In the West, research on dreaming and the popularity of manuals on dream manipulation suggest a revival of interest in an altered state of consciousness that parallels shamanic dreaming. More specifically, the term 'lucid dreaming' has become a passport to newfound freedom in the dream state. It is as though modern individuals, weighed down by the dross of waking life, seek wakefulness in dreaming to reinvigorate their consciousness. The statement, 'Realization that one is dreaming brings a wonderful sense of freedom', represents a liberation not readily discovered in ordinary consciousness.[2] Lucid dreaming is not precisely the same as shamanic dreaming. Although lucid dreaming, like shamanic dreaming, involves an awareness that one is dreaming, it is tied to a notion of the self as a discrete entity embarked on a journey of internal fulfilment. The freedom experienced by lucid dreamers restores the imagination of a self defined by the parameters of modernity. At the same time, lucid dreaming permits a freedom of play that contributes to the postmodern fragmentation of the self. These opposing meanings of freedom in lucid dreaming cannot be found in shamanic dreaming.

The purpose of this chapter is to explore the reinvention of shamanic dreaming as lucid dreaming in the New Age experimentation with altered states of consciousness. Shamanic dreaming often leads to the production of symbols for cultural and social solidarity, whereas lucid dreaming concerns mainly the reconfiguration of the self in a context of re-enchantment. Lucid dreaming has become part of the landscape of signs because it is connected to techniques of re-enchantment that are self-referential and widely marketed. But, like shamanic dreaming, lucid dreaming taps into a reservoir of power that is the immanence of charisma.

The Charisma of Shamanic Dreaming

In modernity, dreaming is clearly distinguished from the experiences of waking life. Dreams are usually regarded as a type of fiction, conjured up by the sleeping mind, that have no direct relationship to waking experiences. Consequently, modern individuals come to think of dreams as symbolizing their fantasies, frustrations and desires. They generally do not treat dream symbolism as a gateway to spiritual knowledge or as a guide to personal behaviour in waking life. For them, dreams function as safety valves to release tensions accumulated in waking consciousness. For example, in his study of nightmares, Mack suggested that 'the nightmare may have served as an "attempt" at psychological integration, not in a conscious or purposive way, but in the employment of fundamental mechanisms available to the organism during sleep for the handling of anxiety and conflict'.[3]

Unlike the modern approach to dreaming, shamanic dreaming in premodern societies entails commitment to a cultural system that emphasizes the continuity between sleep and waking life. Shamans do not dream to release personal tensions, but explore the dream world in order to acquire knowledge for application in waking consciousness. They live in cultural systems that give considerable weight to the religious significance of dreams. In these cultural systems, shamans obtain their power by dreaming. Without dreaming of dead ancestors or spirit familiars, the credibility of the shaman is questioned. Dreaming connects the shaman to other worlds that open up new dimensions of knowledge for healing and personal development in waking life. In the world of shamans, dreaming is an unmistakeable source of power.[4]

Symbols are the basis of shamanic dreaming. They convey special meanings that transform dreams into various types of social action in the waking world. These meanings are religious in the sense that the practical interpretations given to dreams are always framed within a cosmic context. For example, in his interviews with leaders of the Jamaa movement in the Congo, Fabian discovered that it was not possible to understand Jamaa ideology without addressing the religious meaning of dreams. As he put it, 'dreams are called *mawazo* because they make it possible for man to communicate with God and other men beyond the limits set by his body'.[5]

The translation of dream symbols into everyday practices can be interpreted as a specific manipulation of charisma. Since we argued earlier that charisma need not be confined to individuals but is an immanent power in the world, the act of dreaming can indeed be considered an exercise in tapping into the charismatic sources of power beyond the confines of waking life. Particularly in shamanic dreaming, the shaman or the gifted individual enters the dream world as if it were a space of heightened consciousness filled with varieties of knowledge to be utilized in the waking world. Dream knowledge constitutes an expression of immanent charisma because it empowers the shaman to act skilfully and meaningfully when he returns to the world of ordinary consciousness. The skill and meaning attributed to the shaman's dream experiences are derived from his encounters with creative or sacred powers in an altered state of consciousness. The symbols of these dream experiences may become the nucleus of new cultural and religious movements.[6]

Shamanic dreaming is, therefore, an accepted way of attaining extraordinary powers in many traditional societies. It is not an experience that is indiscriminately available to any person, but involves special circumstances for the revelation of magical knowledge to individuals who are chosen or who have the courage to seek it. For example, in Michele Stephen's description of dreaming among the Mekeo of Papua New Guinea, she related a case of a young man who received magical knowledge in his dreams from the spirit of a dead python he found and buried. He learned this technique from his father who instructed him on protection against the risks taken in this quest for power. The Mekeo believed pythons to be dangerous spirit beings.[7]

As a conduit to the immanence of charisma, shamanic dreaming provides the continuity between sleeping and waking by drawing upon cultural symbols to expedite the meanings related to the exercise of power. In other words, the connection between sleeping and waking is made possible by the manipulation of charisma accessed by dreaming. But all these activities take place within a context of cultural symbols that forms the background for the meaningful display of power. Without these symbols, shamanic dreaming could easily lose its effectiveness. In modernity, these symbols are transformed to take on different meanings that sever the continuity between sleeping and waking. Shamanic dreaming then becomes a myth or an anachronism that cannot fit into the modern world of work and technology.

The Self, Modernity and Dreaming

The routines of modern life accentuate the rigours of the waking world over the nebulousness of dreaming. Concern with world mastery implies the need to exert tremendous effort to define reality in terms of concrete achievements in waking consciousness. Hence, the processes of disenchantment promote an attitude of dismissiveness towards shamanic dreaming. The rift between sleeping and waking occasioned by the demands of modern life has reduced the charismatic meaning of dreams found in traditional societies. In modernity, dreams are interpreted as symbols of wish fulfilment rather than as a special medium for the cultivation of power. The sacred nature of shamanic dreaming has no impact in the modern context because it is overwhelmed by the reifying powers of the drive toward world mastery.

Thus, the experience of dreaming in modernity only fascinates poets, scholars and ordinary people looking for the unexpected beyond the routines of waking life. This fascination involves the sense of fluidity associated with the dreaming self in contrast to the bounded roles assumed by the self in waking consciousness. The fleeting identities that punctuate all levels of dreaming provide the self with short-term freedom to pursue all types of innovative action not possible in waking consciousness. In other words, dreams are a source of self-empowerment, filling the gaps created by the harshness of waking realities.

Freud's monumental work on the interpretation of dreams in many ways reflects the problem of the modern self in the twentieth century.[8] Modernity created a peculiar condition in which the quest for freedom was inadvertently defined by the structures of repression. The alleged increase in self-autonomy provided a sense of potential that was not often matched by the conditions of growing inequalities, creeping restrictions and mass surveillance.[9] The modern self sought the very freedom that was denied by its voracious need to control. This was the predicament of the modern self, trapped in an ambivalence that Bauman recognized as an unmistakeable sign of the times: 'Modern existence forces its culture into opposition to itself.'[10] Freud's theory of dreams as wish fulfilment makes sense, then, in this climate of ambivalence. By describing dreams as the 'royal road to the unconscious', Freud was essentially addressing the breakdown of waking identities into a constellation of roles and behavioural expressions that could not be fulfilled in the conscious dimensions of everyday life. What the self could not achieve in a culture of repression became the stuff for expression in the dream world where the limits of modern existence could be transcended.

It is well known that Jung broke away from Freud to formulate his own theory of dreams. He focused on the collective unconscious as a reservoir of symbolic knowledge that seemingly made dreams a special doorway to our inner self. This was a self of vast proportion, greater than the self-identity normally attributed to the actions of waking life. For Jung, not all dreams were the fulfilment of repressed wishes, but, rather, 'their roots lie deep in the unfathomably dark recesses of the conscious mind'. Significant dreams emerged from these dark recesses, characterized by their 'poetic force and beauty'.[11] These particular dreams, according to Jung, were derived from archetypal symbols that transcended all personal experiences. The collective unconscious represents an alternative idea to the constructed nature of the modern social universe. Contrasted with the structure of this universe, the collective unconscious offered a type of authenticity that has no parallel in social reality. It was as though Jung challenged the meaning of self-autonomy in modernity by suggesting that dreaming connected individuals with their symbolic heritage in the collective unconscious.

These modern approaches to dreams and dreaming were not concerned with experiences of sacred empowerment. Rather, the investigation of dreams presented theorists like Freud and Jung with the opportunity to articulate the limits of self-autonomy. Dreams were the template for revealing the hidden nature of the self. The assumption that the modern self possessed the ability to integrate all its experiences as a function of its newfound freedom was undermined by the analysis of dreams. From the psychoanalytic viewpoint, dreams held the key to the dark repressed side of the self. For Jungians, dreams carved a secret path to our primordial being. As a critique of modernity, these different forms of dream analysis challenged the apparent autonomy enjoyed by the self in its quest to control and manage all aspects of waking consciousness. Modernity emphasized the differentiation of waking consciousness to effect the smooth functioning of an organic society. Dream analysis, on the other hand, challenged the functional construction of the modern self by positing the mirror-like nature of dreams that could not be simplistically integrated into the autonomous actions of the modern self. Dreams were fascinating because they called into question our smugness of self-control.

In the 1970s some dream psychologists took the bold move to apply rational control to the world of dreaming.[12] They reasoned that the activation of dream control gave back to individuals the ability to develop self-healing. As an outgrowth of the human potential movement of the 1970s, creative dreaming became a popular form of self-enhancement, which, in a way, challenged the earlier dream theories concerning psychological repression and symbolic domination. Creative dreaming was essentially a response to the idea that self-autonomy was lost in sleep; it was claimed that this autonomy could be restored under conditions of special training and socialization. Both Faraday and Garfield utilized the work of Kilton Stewart to show how this training was possible.[13]

Stewart was an anthropologist who studied the Temiar Senoi, an aboriginal group in peninsular Malaysia, in the 1930s. He claimed from his studies that the Temiar Senoi practised a form of dream control for the purpose of social and cultural integration. This aboriginal group was portrayed as using dreams for self-development, in contrast to Westerners who ignored dreaming as a facet of self-expression and improvement. Stewart was eager to recover this form of knowledge for practical use in Western society. More than 30 years after Stewart published his ideas about

Temiar Senoi dreaming, William Domhoff produced a well-researched critique that raised doubts about such practices and brought to light the Stewart's romantic intentions. Domhoff concluded that:

> The Senoi are indeed nice people, but they do not practice 'Senoi dream theory' as we know it. Kilton Stewart was a well-meaning charmer and storyteller, but in his eagerness to be a prophet, he misunderstood the Senoi and incorrectly attributed his own ideas to them. Senoi dream theory seemed sensible to many Americans during the turbulent sixties, but that is because it combined a new application of traditional American ideas about the malleability of human nature with a story about a lost authenticity.[14]

Domhoff's critique was basically a rebuttal of the modern self in search of meaning beyond waking consciousness. As a dream researcher, he surmised that 'Dreams and dreaming remain largely a mystery to us. We don't know why or when we dream', and he opined that 'Until there is a more systematic body of theory and research on dreams, there may be almost as many dreams as there are dreamers. These dream theories will serve as our mirrors, just as anthropological accounts of tribal peoples often do.'[15] Being sceptical of the claim that creative dreaming is rooted in exotic or lost traditions, Domhoff is in effect drawing out the ambivalence of the modern self in confronting the vicissitudes of everyday life and the allegedly creative wellsprings of the dream world. On the one hand, the modern self is overwhelmed by the problems of everyday life despite the great strides made in science and technology. On the other hand, creative dreaming may provide a panacea for the harshness of waking reality, but we cannot assume that it is removed from the social and cultural contexts of that reality. In other words, the modern self is trapped in a hall of double mirrors: the mirror of being awake and the mirror of dreaming.

Although modernity concerns the effort to attain world mastery, this effort seldom includes the dream world. But creative dreaming, in its attempt to exercise some degree of control in the dream state, could be construed as a derivative of the modern attitude towards mastery of diverse phenomena. Since creative dreaming requires some degree of lucidity in sleep, it raises the question of whether lucid dreaming provides a special condition for increasing self-autonomy in non-waking consciousness, and hence creates an opportunity for a type of self-realization to overcome the ambivalences of the modern world. Domhoff alluded briefly to lucid dreaming as a possible, but under researched, form of dream control.[16] He did not relate lucid dreaming to the question of self-autonomy and the modern context in which this autonomy has become problematic. It is to these issues that we will now turn.

The Ecstasy of Lucid Dreaming

Why lucid dreaming? It was unthinkable for dream theorists like Freud and Jung to ask this question, since they only identified dreaming as a state of consciousness totally different from waking reality. Dreams reflected this reality or, for Jungians, something more universal, but dreams were not considered isomorphic with actions in the waking world because their random occurrence lacked direct self-control. The self in the waking state was assumed to possess rational abilities not found in the dreaming state. It was as though we could only find ourselves after awakening from dreams.

Yet, reports of being awake in dreaming pose critical questions about the nature of the self in non-waking consciousness and the meaning of self-autonomy beyond waking reality. Lucid dreaming refers to self-realization of dreaming and development of control within the dream state. It constitutes an exhilarating experience that purportedly recreates the self as both observer and mover of dream events. The re-creation of the self in lucid dreaming is assumed to affect the constitution of the self in everyday, waking consciousness. By being lucid in the dream state, individuals can allegedly cut through the barrier separating waking and non-waking consciousness to discover a self that possesses an unconditioned freedom of mind. The growing literature on this phenomenon suggests that the attainment of such freedom can alter the conventional meaning of the self.[17]

A taste of this freedom can be gleaned from an account of lucid dreaming by a Dutch physician, Frederik Van Eeden, in the late nineteenth century:

> In the night of January 19–20 [1898], I dreamt that I was lying in the garden before the windows of my study, and saw the eyes of my dog through the glass pane. I was lying on my chest and observing the dog very keenly. At the same time, however, I knew with perfect certainty that I was dreaming and lying on my back in my bed. And then I resolved to wake up slowly and carefully and observe how my sensation of lying on my chest would change into the sensation of lying on my back. And so I did, slowly and deliberately, and the transition – which I have since undergone many times – is most wonderful. It is like slipping from one body into another, and there is distinctly a *double* recollection of the two bodies.[18]

Van Eeden's description of his experience in lucid dreaming gives the impression that the self of the lucid dreamer is highly fluid and not subjected to the rules that govern the conditioning of the self in waking reality. Freedom in lucid dreaming implies a high degree of self-transformability that cannot be replicated in waking life. It is this freedom of transformability that expands the meaning of self-autonomy.

The modern self seeks to increase its autonomy in the waking world to establish its sense of control over as many empirical objects as possible. But we argued in Chapter 1 that the ambivalences of modernity instantiate the possibility of self-destruction and thus curb the very freedom valued by the self. In lucid dreaming, this freedom is restored by the ability of the self to confront the malleability of its own identity. The paradox of knowing that one is awake in a dream provides the special condition for realizing the illusory nature of all identities. This realization frees the self to experience all phenomenal fabrications as expressions of its own creative powers.

In Celia Green's pioneering work on lucid dreams, she showed that freedom of transformability could be applied to affect the course of actual dreaming. For example, she reported the case of a person who dreamt he was shot dead, but was sufficiently lucid to replay the dream sequence to the point of neutralizing the stressful effects.[19] This example suggests a specific relationship between lucid dreaming and self-autonomy that enhances the potential for therapeutic transformations. The fluidity of the self in lucid dreaming provides the means for tapping into these transformations that are not always possible in the waking world. But to realize this fluidity in lucid dreaming implies that the self can be rediscovered in the waking world to be a storehouse of unlimited potential.

The quest for mastery of self-consciousness in dreaming, therefore, constitutes a prelude to the realization of the continuity of self-transformation between the waking and non-waking worlds. The attainment of this realization for the modern self suggests the possibility of overcoming the unsettling experiences of modern existence. Indeed, there is a sense of anti-Freudianism in lucid dreaming because the self consciously refutes the influence of repressed wishes by confronting the dream state as an extrapolation of waking identity. Dreams now become the medium in which the self negotiates the meaning of variability in waking life. By being lucid in dreams, the self is not only able to manipulate dream events but also to integrate the continuum between waking and sleeping.

The techniques for attaining dream lucidity are now available in various popular books and manuals[20] providing detailed descriptions of lucid dream experiences and specific instructions on how to attain them. Written largely for the general public, the authors of these books seem to imply that every individual has the capability to experience lucid dreaming. They suggest that, given the right motivation, every individual can become lucid in dreaming. However, certain techniques have to be learned as basic steps in attaining dream lucidity. First, a systematic recording of dreams in a journal is necessary as a method of disciplining the self to recall as many dreams as possible and their details. It is assumed that unless the self is able to remember dreams, lucid dreaming will not be easily achieved. This type of self-discipline provides the aspiring lucid dreamer with a routine to soften the boundary between waking and sleeping. By recalling and recording dreams, the individual is made to pay as much attention to dream events as he or she would to waking events.

The recognition of dream signs is the second technique for gaining lucidity in the dream state. Dream signs are distinctive events that occur frequently in dreams and are recognized by the individual as possible indications for becoming conscious in dreaming. According to LaBerge and Rhinegold, 'dreamsigns can be like neon lights, flashing a message in the darkness: This is a dream! This is a dream!'[21] In their view, every dream contains personal dream signs that can be deduced from the recordings in a dream journal. LaBerge gives the example of his mutant contact lens that multiples as a personal dream sign.[22] His advice to catalogue dream signs comprises another form of self-discipline to penetrate the fog that surrounds the dreamer.

These basic techniques suggest that the self can be motivated and taught to become conscious while dreaming. Familiarity with these techniques implies that the self need not be a 'prisoner' of dreams, but can directly take charge of dreaming to expand the horizon of consciousness. Naturally, mastery of these techniques takes time. Many people may not be able to recognize dream signs immediately, or they may keep missing them in their dreams.

The maintenance of focus in dreams is not necessarily dependent on specific techniques, but can be an outcome of self-exertion – that is, the exertion of willpower. It means that self-determination to actualize the state of awareness in dreaming can induce lucidity. LaBerge and Rhinegold believe that a person's will can be strengthened as part of his or her training towards attainment of dream lucidity.[23] The use of willpower to induce lucid dreaming suggests that any person can initiate dreaming if he or she is fully committed to gaining such experiences.

In shamanic dreaming, however, the shaman's will plays a different role. Since the shaman is considered chosen to receive dreaming powers, he does not apply his will in the same way that an ordinary person uses his will to initiate lucid dreaming. The shaman's dreams come to him naturally, but he may apply his will to control the dreaming process just as he would in a trance of magical flight.[24] The shaman's connection to the dream world is not the same as that of someone who engages in lucid dreaming. As a person chosen to receive dreaming powers, the shaman enters the dream world to seek specific knowledge in order to benefit others in the waking world. In other words, the shaman is a vehicle of dream knowledge not accessible to ordinary people. Lucid dreamers, on the other hand, may not be specifically seeking dream knowledge for thaumaturgy in the waking world. The experiences gained by lucid dreamers tend to be utilized for self-understanding. Knowledge of lucid dreaming may be published and shared, but it is generally for sensitizing people to the significance of dream consciousness and training them to be alert in the dream state.

Yet, shamanic dreaming and lucid dreaming converge as forms of ecstasy beyond the structures of disenchantment. In shamanic dreaming, the power to communicate with deities and other beings propels the shaman into an ecstatic state that brings about profound changes in visualization, feelings and consciousness. Similarly, lucid dreamers experience ecstasy as high states of perception, although they do not necessarily communicate with beings from other worlds. These states of perception vary in intensity, but LaBerge asserts that the average lucid dream is perceptually more vivid than the average non-lucid dream.[25] Ecstasy in both shamanic and lucid dreaming suggests that dreaming under these special conditions provides entry into the immanence of charisma. The heightened sense of perception and expanded consciousness in shamanic and lucid dreaming are not dissimilar to the experience of charismatic empowerment. The ability to consciously transcend or exceed physical limitations in these dream states indicates that the shaman and lucid dreamer share a portal into the charismatic transformation of reality. In the case of lucid dreaming, LaBerge even suggested that it 'could allow people to learn to live in any imaginable world; to experience and better choose among various possible futures'.[26]

The charismatic link between shamanic and lucid dreaming makes it possible to address the emerging popularity of lucid dreaming as a type of re-enchantment that attempts to recover the continuity between waking and sleeping. Increasing receptivity to the notion that the dream state comprises a reality not unlike the waking state is evidenced by the growing number of seminars, workshops and books on the subject. Techniques in controlled dreaming constitute a growing fascination with the unexplored aspects of human consciousness. They also represent a type of rebellion against the disenchanted view of dreams as unreal. A dream industry is emerging from the New Age preoccupation with the immanence of charisma in all states of human consciousness. It is an industry that seeks to empower the individual self, through a variety of dreaming techniques, to awaken in the dream state and experience an uninhibited expansion of consciousness.

The re-enchantment of dreams transcends religious boundaries. Practitioners of lucid dreaming are not always or exclusively identified with specific religious traditions, although some may base their dreaming experiences and expertise on a religious tradition known for its practices of controlled dreaming (for example, the Tibetan Bön and Buddhist tradition).[27] Because lucid dreaming is not strictly a religious property or claimed by stalwarts of a particular religion, it is readily adaptable to the conditions of New Age experimentation. In the postmodern West, both the conditions of consciousness exploration and marketed innovations coincide with a demand for re-enchanted experiences in dreaming. Freed from religious influences, these conditions facilitate research into lucid dreaming that requires no religious commitments and promotes the use of advanced technology for exploring dream states. Lucid dreaming has now entered a new phase that brings together the application of Western technology in consciousness research and the subtlety of movements in the dream world. What makes lucid dreaming unique at the beginning of the twenty-first century is its systematization for a mass market of practitioners. To understand the packaging of dream practices, we will compare the approaches of two contemporary dream researchers.

The New Shamans of Dreaming

Ann Faraday is a London-trained psychologist with research experiences in hypnotherapy. As a pioneer of the human potential movement, she invested much energy in charting dream territories for the positive development of the human mind. Her first popular book on dreams was written to inspire people to take their dreams seriously and to apply them in their daily lives.[28] After the success of her first book, she wrote a second book in response to the increasing public interest in learning to understand and interpret dreams.[29]

Faraday's approach to dreaming circumvents the classic Freudian paradigm of dream analysis. Whereas Freud saw the dream state as an ideal symbolic cover for various forms of aggressive and instinctual behaviour, Faraday treated dreams as an open book containing symbolic language that was 'no different from the metaphorical and slang expressions we use all the time in waking life'.[30] She abandoned Freudian dream theory for a more pragmatic approach that related the dynamics of dreaming to personal symbols. For her, dream interpretation was a type of self-discovery based on a personal understanding of the immediate circumstances in which dream symbols operated. Hence, it was not appropriate for dream therapists to 'force their own trip on the dreamer'.[31] In short, the dream game implied that each individual was autonomous in evaluating the symbolic meanings of his or her dreams.

To make the dream game accessible to the general public, Faraday discussed a wide range of dream themes and symbols that were pragmatically related to the dreamers' personal lives. She brought these symbols from the depths of the unconscious to the surfaces of everyday life, in order to demystify the apparently arcane nature of dreaming. For example, dreams of nudity were not necessarily interpreted as sexual but as concerns with one's vulnerability in life.[32] Her method of dream interpretation would seem to suggest that she had not really departed from a disenchanted framework that removed all magic from dreaming. Dreaming was just another way of making sense of, or coming to terms with, our mundane lives.

However, the shamanic element in her work on dreaming becomes evident in her treatment of nightmares, especially in the way a dreamer utilizes awareness in dreams to combat personal fears. Her method of resolving nightmares by dream manipulation does not differ radically from the classic ritual of shamanic initiation, which emphasizes confrontation with enemies, illnesses and various powerful forces in the dream state.[33] She herself once dreamed that she was pursued by some murderous Eskimos. When she realized that it was only a dream, she turned to face her enemies and dared them to kill her. She looked away while they stabbed her dream body. When it was over, she laughed at their futile efforts and they walked away sheepishly.[34] She had used her lucidity in dreaming as a technique to overcome fear – a central emotion to be grappled with and tamed, before a person could traditionally qualify as a shaman.

According to her account, not only did she use lucid dreaming to quell her dream enemies, but she also employed Don Juan's technique of lucid dreaming to stabilize dream images[35] described earlier in our discussion of Carlos Castaneda in Chapter 5 and involving the ability to stabilize the image of the hands and then shift this focus to various objects in the dream environment. This was another instance of her use of classic shamanic training in order to gain mastery over an altered state of consciousness.

Thus, Faraday took personal experiences in dreaming to construct a practical guide for understanding dream symbolism, but at the same time she introduced her readers to the possibility of playing the dream game by actively manipulating those symbols. However, the act of manipulating dream symbols was merely recounted as a self-generated power that might lead to greater freedom of consciousness. In other words, her approach straddled the disenchanted world of dream interpretation for mundane living and the re-enchanted world of shamanic dreaming for extraordinary experiences. It was an approach that required a shift in attitude towards dreaming as a significant aspect of living and an intention to develop a sense of wakefulness in the dream state. No hard technology was applied in her approach to dreaming.

More than a decade later, the work of Stephen LaBerge changed the dreamscape of bourgeois consciousness. Trained in mathematics, physics and psychophysiology, LaBerge took some of the findings of sleep research conducted at Stanford University and applied them to the manipulation of the dream state. The results of his research, as well as instructions for attaining lucidity in the dream state, were published in two bestsellers.[36]

Like Faraday, LaBerge does not adhere to a Freudian theory of dreams. Unlike Faraday, LaBerge goes beyond dream symbolism to explicate the means by which a person could take charge of his or her own dreams. He emphasizes personal intent in exploring dreamscapes, thus disclosing a strong shamanic concern with the empowerment of consciousness in the dream state. LaBerge himself began training in the art of dreaming by attending workshops given by Tarthang Tulku in the early 1970s.[37] With profound simplicity, his teacher addressed everything around him as a dream. LaBerge has incorporated this teaching into his method of de-differentiating between waking and dreaming experiences. For example, he tells his readers who are practising to become lucid dreamers to imagine that 'all things are of the substance of dreams'.[38] With many years of personal experiences in lucid dreaming and scientific research on the dream state, he is able to systematically provide detailed instructions on, as well as empirical explanations for, the induction of lucid dreaming.

LaBerge has no explicit links to the world of shamans. Yet, the practices in lucid dreaming that he teaches are not inconsistent with the basic approaches to shamanic dreaming. For instance, he instructs his readers to look for dream signs that provide clues to the peculiarities of the dream state.[39] As described earlier, dream signs are compared to neon lights in the dark. By keeping a dream journal in which a person records his or her dreams on a regular basis, personal dream signs can be recognized and applied in dreaming in order to attain lucidity. Similarly, in the technique that Don Juan taught Castaneda, the hands were treated as dream signs to direct the dreamer's attention to the state of dreaming.

In addition to dream signs, LaBerge teaches his readers to move directly into the dreaming stage by falling asleep consciously.[40] This method, known as the Wake-Initiated Lucid Dreams (WILDS), dissolves the boundaries between waking and dreaming consciousness by using the onset of sleep as an opening into the dream state. The principal technique in WILDS relates to focusing attention on various objects and images while falling asleep without losing consciousness of unfolding events. LaBerge introduces his readers to some Tibetan Buddhist approaches to WILDS that incorporate yogic breathing and visualization. He refers to the method taught by Tarthang Tulku that emphasizes the visualization of a flame in the lotus centred in the throat – a region of the body believed by Tibetan Buddhists to be associated with dreaming.[41]

Much effort and will are required for aspiring lucid dreamers to experience the fruits of their practices. Knowing this, LaBerge has gone on to use his scientific research on sleep and dreaming to produce special techniques for facilitating entry into the world of lucid dreaming. By establishing the Lucidity Institute in Stanford, California, LaBerge and his team of researchers are able to promote research on lucid dreaming and market the special technologies from their research to members of the public who are interested in advancing their abilities in lucid dreaming.[42]

The main function of these technologies is to provide an externally produced signal that induces awareness of dreaming and possibly may help dreamers hasten their initial experiences of lucid dreaming. By using the DreamLight, a miniature biofeedback computer with sensing instruments to detect REM sleep,[43] dreamers are alerted to their being in the dream state by a cue (a flashing light and/or a sound) through a sleep mask. LaBerge has reported that some DreamLight users interpreted the cues as part of the dream scene, such as pulsations or unusual illuminations. Almost immediately, they became aware that they were dreaming.[44]

Other innovative devices developed by LaBerge and his colleagues include the DreamSpeaker, the NovaDreamer and the SuperNovaDreamer. The DreamSpeaker plays a digitally recorded message during REM sleep to induce recognition of the dream state. The NovaDreamer contains infrared sensors that detect rapid eye movements, whereupon pre-set patterns of light and sound are sent to the dreamer to induce lucidity. The SuperNovaDreamer is a NovaDreamer device that is connected to a personal computer to enhance the controls for lucid dreaming.[45]

All these technological developments have taken the art of dreaming beyond the level of symbolic interpretation. Dreamers who gain lucidity through these technological innovations are more likely to be concerned with their newly acquired ability to manipulate the dream state than to make symbolic sense of dream events. In other words, LaBerge has transformed the symbolic approach to shamanic dreaming into a high-tech manipulation of signs in the dream state. The development of sophisticated technological devices to induce lucid dreaming suggests that individuals are no longer dependent on the exclusive power of a teacher or virtuoso to activate their ability to manipulate dreams. They can undertake this task themselves in a manner that brings together technological knowledge and creative self-effort to solve problems and heal the inner self.

Dreaming in the New Age

From Faraday to LaBerge, dreaming has taken on the characteristics of a popular culture devoted to self-empowerment. It is this culture that defines the New Age not as a remarkably special era for discovering the continuity of magic, but as an underestimated current of dissatisfaction with the insipidity of the real, the mundane and the ordinary. The New Age constitutes an attempt to prise open the submerged powers of the modern, sedate self. Indeed, this self strives to seek re-enchantment by turning to the irrational for charismatic inspiration. As Tiryakian expressed it, since the nineteenth century, themes of 'the fantastic, the imaginary, the grotesque, the mythic' have infused modern consciousness to give the self a sense of liberation from the vapid routines of modern life.[46]

Within the logic of modern differentiation, dreams cannot be construed as continuous with the realities of waking life. Thus, the whole tradition of dream interpretation, most eminently represented by the Freudian school, revolved around an enclosed set of symbols that were not 'real' in themselves, but reflected inner desires played out in the unassuming confines of everyday life. Dreams were seen as the surfacing in sleep of inner thoughts, unfulfilled desires and unresolved conflicts, taking on a form that could not have any real bearing on the actions of waking life. We could only read our dreams; we could not make them equivalent to our waking lives.

On the other hand, traditional shamans treat the dream world as inseparable from the world of waking consciousness. They impose no fixed definitions of reality on either the world of waking or dreaming, but they do view the ability to navigate the dream world as a special power that enhances personal perception of, and interaction in, waking life. Hence, they use the power of dreams for guidance and healing in the mundane world. Similarly, New Age shamans also approach dreaming as a source of power for healing and managing the vicissitudes of daily life. They, too, attribute to lucid dreaming the signs of overcoming the division between dreaming and waking consciousness.

Unlike traditional shamans, New Age shamans use modern technology and the mass media to disseminate their knowledge of dreaming to a mass audience eager to seek new transformations in their lives. In the context of technological innovations and electronic dissemination of information, New Age shamans are able to package instructions effectively and rapidly for practitioners of lucid dreaming. Thus, the popularization of lucid dreaming is not only breaking down the symbols of dream interpretation, but also embedding the dream game in a sign culture that commoditizes the search for authentic experiences.

As discussed in Chapter 3, the New Age movement transacts signs rather than symbols in a social milieu that is not hostile to re-enchantment as an item of consumption in everyday life. Within this milieu, the self is experienced as a free-floating agent that has no centre, but is open to myriad encounters with sign-related phenomena. In short, the New Age movement promotes lives of multiple identities that can be taken on without inhibition in shamanic dreaming. Lucidity in shamanic dreaming predisposes the dreamer to be conscious of the freedom to change identities at will. Under these conditions, the self experiences a type of conscious fluidity that makes dreaming an art of empowerment without the restrictions of symbolic interpretation. A person can be who he or she wants to be in the dream state. By recognizing certain signs in the dream state, a dreamer can attain a lucidity that intensifies the ability to manipulate identities.

The mass availability of dreaming devices, such as those invented by LaBerge, suggests that the path to lucid dreaming can take a more technological and less personal form. In this sense, the symbolic approach to dreaming may disappear into the power of the masses. At the level of the masses, the power of conscious dreaming becomes attached to the regime of the sign. This is a regime that is antithetical to fixed boundaries, just as lucid dreaming shatters all boundaries of the self. Unencumbered by symbolic meanings, lucid dreaming, under the regime of the sign, takes re-enchantment deep into the heart of bourgeois consciousness.

As argued in Chapter 3, bourgeois consciousness has for a long time yielded to the alienating conditions of modernity. The self became a disparate entity, far removed from the phenomenal world of which it was a part. The New Age movement changed all that by redefining the sacred as a power within each individual to experience the undifferentiated nature of all phenomena. It introduced seekers to the immanence of charisma by connecting the signs of liberation through a vast network of movements that emphasized the exploration of untapped human potential. Thus, the exploration of lucid dreaming represents an important breakthrough in the way in which bourgeois consciousness reconciles the self with the objects of its experiences. In lucid dreaming, self-awareness of the dream state promotes the dissolution of boundaries between the self and dream objects.

In a sense, lucid dreaming is a de-alienating experience that restores holistic consciousness as well as reduces dualistic perception.

With the aid of innovative dream technologies, bourgeois consciousness is able to move beyond the taint and excesses of the psychedelic 1960s.[47] In contrast to the hallucinogenic ecstasies of the 1960s, high-tech lucid dreaming provides drug-free, controlled encounters with an altered state of consciousness. Lucid dreaming in the New Age is, therefore, a sophisticated form of shamanic dreaming that may gradually change the way in which bourgeois consciousness has symbolically dealt with the realms of the subconscious and the unconscious. It has the potential to transform traditional shamanism into a postmodern practice that reconfigures the definition of reality.

Lucid dreaming in the New Age can be construed as the reshaping of shamanism under the regime of the sign. This does not imply that lucid dreaming is just another form of escapism. Rather, it is an expansion of consciousness through the de-differentiation of waking and sleeping. The public can now access this type of consciousness expansion because of the availability of various dream technologies, the marketing of which embeds lucid dreaming in the culture of signs. Signs make dreaming in the New Age different from the traditional understanding of dreams as esoteric symbols of the mind. Whereas the symbolic system is crucial in traditional shamanic dreaming, signs are the guideposts in contemporary lucid dreaming. Unlike shamans who must interpret their dreams within an established symbolic system, lucid dreamers treat all dream experiences as self-referential. Signs in lucid dreaming are not only clues to self-awakening in dreams, but they are also arbitrary codes for self-identity in dreaming.

The popularization of lucid dreaming suggests that re-enchantment can occur without the need for religious affiliations. Lucid dreaming transacts all possibilities of identity formation as signs of re-enchantment rather than as symbols of religious salvation. It does not mean that lucid dreaming as a New Age activity will eventually replace established forms of institutional religiosity. As an alternative form of consciousness enhancement, lucid dreaming restores the transformability of the self in a way that could challenge the institutional parameters of self-identity. But religious identities linked to institutional forms in the waking world cannot be instantly erased by the fluid experiences of lucid dreaming. Since these identities are related to public symbols of group formation, they can reify the individual sense of belonging in a specific community and relegate the autonomy of lucid dreaming to the private realm. In this realm, lucid dreaming can be considered a 'new religion' in the sense that it has roots in shamanic dreaming and its charm lies in the New Age romance of creativity – the belief in the ability to remake one's self without institutional constraints. For this reason, lucid dreaming will continue to fascinate seekers across religious boundaries and direct the process of re-enchantment towards the expansion of consciousness.

Notes

1 Mircea Eliade (1964), *Shamanism: Archaic Techniques of Ecstasy*, Princeton, NJ: Princeton University Press, p.103.
2 Charles McCreery (1973), *Psychical Phenomena and the Physical World*, London: Hamish Hamilton, p.114.
3 John E. Mack (1974), *Nightmares and Human Conflict*, Boston: Houghton Mifflin, p.233.
4 For accounts of shamanic dreaming, see Eliade, *Shamanism*, *op.cit.*, Chapter 2.
5 Johannes Fabian (1966), 'Dreams and Charisma: "Theories of Dreams" in the Jamaa-Movement (Congo)', *Anthropos*, 61, pp.544–60 at p.559.
6 See Vittorio Lanternari (1975), 'Dreams as Charismatic Significants: Their Bearing on the Rise of New Religious Movements', in T.R. Williams (ed.), *Psychological Anthropology*, The Hague: Mouton, pp.221–35.
7 Michele Stephen (1982), 'Dreaming is Another Power: The Social Significance of Dreams Among the Mekeo of Papua New Guinea', *Oceania*, 53(2), pp.106–22.
8 Sigmund Freud (1954), *The Interpretation of Dreams*, London: Allen and Unwin.
9 See Michel Foucault (1977), *Discipline and Punish*, Harmondwsorth: Penguin; Anthony Giddens (1990), *The Consequences of Modernity*, Cambridge: Polity Press.
10 Zygmunt Bauman (1990), 'Modernity and Ambivalence', in M. Featherstone (ed.), *Global Culture*, London: Sage, pp.143–70 at p.166.
11 Carl G. Jung (1974), *Dreams*, Princeton, NJ: Princeton University Press, pp.73, 77.
12 Ann Faraday (1974), *Dream Power*, London: Pan; and idem (1976), *The Dream Game*, Harmondsworth: Penguin; Patricia Garfield (1974), *Creative Dreaming*, New York: Ballantine Books.
13 Kilton Stewart (1972),'Dream Theory in Malaya', in C.T. Tart (ed.), *Altered States of Consciousness*, New York: Anchor Books, pp.161–70.
14 G. William Domhoff (1985), *The Mystique of Dreams*, Berkeley, CA: University of California Press, p.96.
15 Ibid., pp.114, 117.
16 Ibid., pp.89–90.
17 See Celia E. Green (1968), *Lucid Dreams*, London: Hamish Hamilton; Stephen LaBerge (1985), *Lucid Dreaming*, New York: Ballantine Books; Celia E. Green and Charles McCreery (1994), *Lucid Dreaming*, London: Routledge; Robert Moss (1996), *Conscious Dreaming*, New York: Crown Publishing Group.
18 Frederik Van Eeden (1972), 'A Study of Dreams', in C.T. Tart (ed.), *Altered States of Consciousness*, New York: Anchor Books, pp.147–60.
19 Green, *Lucid Dreams*, *op.cit.*, p.46.
20 See Keith Harary and Pamela Weintraub (1989), *Lucid Dreams in 30 Days*, New York: St Martin's Press; Stephen LaBerge and Howard Rhinegold (1990), *Exploring the World of Lucid Dreaming*, New York: Ballantine Books.
21 LaBerge and Rhinegold, *Exploring the World of Lucid Dreaming*, *op.cit.*, p.41
22 Ibid., p.42.
23 Ibid., pp.307–11.
24 See Larry Peters and Douglass Price-Williams (1980), 'Towards an Experiential Analysis of Shamanism', *American Ethnologist*, 7, pp.397–418.
25 See Stephen LaBerge and Donald J. DeGracia (2000), "Varieties of Lucid Dreaming Experience', in R.G. Kunzendorf and B. Wallace (eds), *Individual Differences in Conscious Experience*, Amsterdam: John Benjamins, pp.269–307.
26 Stephen LaBerge (1993), 'Lucidity Research, Past and Future', *NightLight*, 5(3), p.6.
27 See Tenzin Wangyal Rinpoche (1998), *The Tibetan Yogas of Dream and Sleep*, Ithaca, NY: Snow Lion.
28 Ann Faraday (1974), *Dream Power*, London: Pan.
29 Ann Faraday (1976), *The Dream Game*, Harmondsworth,: Penguin.

30 Ibid., p.62.
31 Ibid., p.12.
32 Ibid., pp.76–7.
33 See Eliade, *Shamanism*, *op.cit.*, p.33ff.
34 Faraday, *The Dream Game*, p.224.
35 Ibid., p.284.
36 LaBerge, *Lucid Dreaming*, *op.cit.*; LaBerge and Rhinegold, *Exploring the World of Lucid Dreaming*, *op.cit.*
37 LaBerge and Rhinegold, *Exploring the World of Lucid Dreaming*, *op.cit.*, p.67. Tarthang Tulku is from the Nyingma sect of Tibetan Buddhism that has close ties to the shamanic Bön religion of ancient Tibet.
38 Ibid., p.67.
39 Ibid., pp.40–47.
40 Ibid., Chapter 4.
41 Ibid., pp.100–106.
42 The Lucidity Institute has a membership list and conducts training programmes in lucid dreaming. It also publishes a newsletter, *NightLight*. Information on its activities can be accessed through the website <www.lucidity.com>.
43 A stage of sleep comprising patterns of rapid eye movement (REM) that are associated with dreaming activities.
44 LaBerge and Rhinegold, *Exploring the World of Lucid Dreaming*, *op.cit.*, pp.90–91.
45 Articles on these devices can be found in Keelin (1995), 'Adventures with the NovaDreamer', *NightLight* 7(1); Stephen LaBerge and Brenda Giguere (1995), 'Pillow Talk: Announcing the DreamSpeaker', *NightLight* 7(2); Lynne Levitan (1996), 'Introducing the *Super*NovaDreamer', *NightLight* 8(1–2). These devices can be purchased through the Lucidity Institute's website.
46 Edward A. Tiryakian (1992), 'Dialectics of Modernity: Reenchantment and Dedifferentiation as Counterprocesses', in H. Haferkamp and N.J. Smelser (eds), *Social Change and Modernity*, Berkeley, CA: University of California Press, pp.85–6.
47 The psychedelic 1960s not only defined drug-taking as an act of rebellion against authority, but also as a route to alternative realities. It was a period that brought together the power of hallucinogenic drugs and revolutionary politics. See Timothy Leary (1970), *The Politics of Ecstasy*, London: Paladin; Todd Gitlin (1993), *The Sixties: Years of Hope, Days of Rage*, New York: Bantam Books.

Chapter 7

The Consequences of Re-enchantment

When Baudrillard declared that God has departed but left his judgement behind, he ironically echoed the classic statement on disenchantment.[1] The world was no longer seen as being under the influence of sacred or supernatural forces. God's judgement merely represented abstract principles to be interpreted and contested over by different groups and individuals in society. Social power replaced the belief in the immanence of charisma. Religious experiences in a disenchanted world were constituted by a hegemonic relationship between ecclesiastical orders that claimed mediation of the divine will and neophytes who submitted to their authority. What became disenchanted were not so much the magical and charismatic worldviews of the masses, but the rechannelling of those beliefs into specific structures of power maintained exclusively by representatives of the ecclesiastical orders. This was the instrumental view of disenchantment offered by Weber who saw 'sacramental' or 'corporate grace' as the ritual property of the priesthood and not of the lay individual.[2]

In other words, the restricted access to magical power provided the impression of a reduced public concern with the workings of the supernatural. Hierocratic management of this power presupposed a form of rationalization in which specific roles were developed for the dispensation of charisma. Within the confines of these roles, arcane knowledge was incorporated into well-defined rituals that came to embody the basis of established religion. These rituals no longer possessed the outer trappings of magical practices. This was what Keith Thomas meant when he said that religion 'had a multi-dimensional character which gave it an importance which contemporary magical beliefs could never rival. They lacked its institutional framework, its systematic theology, its moral code and its wide range of social functions'.[3]

Thus, disenchantment was a process of distancing, differentiating, as it did, the realm of magic from the realm of the secular and mundane. Magical powers were either coopted into the formal rituals of ecclesiastical orders or redefined as the underground activities of mystical movements. In time to come, the rise of Western science even overshadowed the formal rituals of ecclesiastical orders by promoting the idea that what was yielded by scientific work was 'worth being known'.[4] This led Weber to conclude that '[o]ne need no longer have recourse to magical means in order to master or implore the spirits.... Technical means and calculations perform the service'.[5]

Given the negative consequences of disenchantment for the promulgation of an undifferentiated magical cosmos, it would seem logical to conceive re-enchantment as the restoration of charismatic meaning in a world disillusioned by the iron cages of modern progress. Yet, re-enchantment is not a straightforward process of mobilizing the magical. Unlike the emergence of disenchantment in the era of modern symbols, re-enchantment in the contemporary world is unfolding under the influence of the sign. Disenchantment in modernity involved the fragmentation of symbolic power. The differentiation of science from magic implied the separation of symbolic realms. Each realm constituted its own source of representation in world mastery. The symbols of science represented the prestige and domination of systematic empirical knowledge for gaining exact control of the external world. The symbols of magic, on the other hand, represented a type of covert knowledge that precluded the meaning of falsifiability in the manipulation of the external world. In the process of disenchantment, scientific symbols gained more credibility over magical ones, but left some room for re-enchantment to occur as a form of entertainment (like sci-fi, fantasy horror, and so on) that offered no serious threat to the scientific enterprise. Under the regime of the symbol, re-enchantment was not disruptive of disenchantment, but exemplified the subordination of the magical realm to the scientific one.

However, re-enchantment under the sign is occurring at a time when the realm of science is no longer considered an unequivocal field of inquiry that adjudicates all meanings of reality. This is not to say that science has lost its ground of influence but that scientific symbols are no longer held in thrall for representing all aspects of reality.[6] For this reason, scientific symbols have to compete with signs to define reality. In the system of the sign, reality is not readily constituted by symbols of prestige and deference, but by the experience of authenticity and efficacy in dealing with the immediate situation. The symbolic mediation of this experience becomes unwarranted because direct contact captures the profundity of sensory manifestations more effectively. For example, cybertechnology has introduced scientific researchers to interactive graphical simulations (IGS) that facilitate direct sensory contact with the objects of research.[7] The use of IGS in science does not necessarily spell the end of symbolic representation in scientific research. Rather, it enhances the meaning and significance of immediate experience in scientific endeavours. Similarly, the development of technology for actualizing lucid dreaming (described in the previous chapter) promotes direct sensory manipulation of dreams rather than their symbolic interpretation.

The advent of the sign system, therefore, provides a levelling effect on all realms of experience. Direct experience with minimal or no representation is the signifying route to reducing all forms of symbolic differentiation. Under the regime of the sign, the realms of science and magic are not ranged against each other in terms of authenticity, since experiential continuity from one realm to the next tends to break down the meaning of hegemonic reality. Re-enchantment under the sign revives the significance of magic not only as a domain of direct experiential power, but also as a practice that is not necessarily subordinate to that of science.

Nevertheless, the re-enchanted self in the sign system confronts a paradoxical situation in which the revival of magic may not be exclusively directed towards a reconstruction of the self but possibly towards its obliteration. The romance of irrationality that advanced bourgeois definitions of mystical autonomy and individual creativity was based on symbolic notions of selfhood addressing the limits of disenchantment. As pointed out in Chapter 3, Western romantics sought re-enchantment as a form of symbolic resistance to industrial capitalist civilization. This resistance provided a strategy for renewing the meaning of the self in a highly mechanized world that was seen to rob the self of its dignity and spontaneity. Romanticism was the self's last stand against its engulfment by the symbols of modern progress.

But in the age of the sign, romanticism cannot easily maintain its autonomous position as the defender of the self. It is the arbitrary nature of the sign that undermines romantic certitude of the self's inherent existence. Signs do not relate to anything except to themselves, and so they cannot point invariably to any single object of reference. This implies that signs are by nature a poor guide to firm meanings. In effect, signs can possibly destabilize any meaning that is developed for the realization of the self. Because the sign has a disabling effect on self-interpretation, re-enchantment within the context of the sign is not intrinsically a process of self-affirmation. The re-enchanted self assumes that the rediscovery of magic and charisma can lift it to greater heights of meaning, promising some form of ontological salvation. Instead, the signs of re-enchantment point only to other signs without necessarily addressing the need to prop up self-images.

The encroachment of the sign on the symbol signals the emergence of a decentred cosmos in which the self is left to falter in the wake of experiential contingencies. The re-enchantment of religion in such a cosmos suggests that religious structures founded on symbolic interaction can be transformed into commodities of salvation, which empower a quest for myriad charismatic experiences. The emphasis on immediacy, spontaneity and novelty fragments, rather than augments, the symbolic integrity of the self. To know and experience other worlds through re-enchantment is to break down the symbolic constitution of the self into moments of sign-filled ecstasy. The fluid experiences of lucid dreaming exemplify such ecstatic moments. The paradoxical effect of being awake in dreams not only problematizes the meaning of self-identity but also enhances the power of uninterrupted consciousness, a source of charismatic experiences.

The quest for charismatic experiences may lead to a less rigorous concern for the actualization of the symbolic self. In the extreme case, physical annihilation through a collectively arranged act of self-destruction reroutes the meaning of re-enchantment into the realm of death. Mass annihilation in religious movements points to a collective rejection of self-renewal within the symbolic boundaries of social existence. To die with the leader and other members is more than a symbolic act of defiance against the rational conventions of social decency and self-preservation. It highlights self-destruction as the final stage in the quest for transcendence of disenchantment. For instance, the mass suicide of followers in religious movements such as People's Temple, Temple of the Solar Order, and Heaven's Gate suggests that the death of the self may possibly be the ultimate sign of re-enchantment.[8]

On the other hand, the disappearance of the self through the realization of the self's illusory nature is not, by definition, an act of self-destruction but of deep insight. Such an insight has become possible because of Western re-enchantment with views on 'emptiness' in religions such as Buddhism.[9] The meaning of 'emptiness' has become more significant for understanding the fragmentation of the self in postmodernism. In addressing this problem, Clarke pointed out that Asian thought 'has proved to be able to offer a provocative external perspective, and the idea that the self is not given by nature but constructed, not stable and permanent but painfully fractured, is one which has drawn contemporary concerns close to traditional teachings of Buddhism'.[10] He also asserted that the concept of 'emptiness' associated with the philosophical works of Nagarjuna, the second-century Buddhist thinker, has become the subject of growing interest in the West.[11]

Through contact with Buddhist concept of 'emptiness', individuals may come to realize the self as a fragile symbolic construction and not an entity existing on its own terms. It may enable the absorption of the self into a decentred cosmos as a sign of liberation. Thus, re-enchantment in the contemporary West suggests a process of reversal in which the symbols of disenchantment that reified the self are transformed into signs that dissolve the self. The dissolution of the self does not imply that 'emptiness' is equivalent to nothingness. On the contrary, the arbitrariness of signs contributes to an understanding of 'emptiness' as the inherent potential of consciousness to reproduce itself in myriad ways. The centrality of the self is undermined by the insouciant nature of signs, thus disclosing the permeability of all identities.

However, in Asia, re-enchantment is not really meaningful because disenchantment there has yet to reach its zenith in order for a process of reversal to occur. Although large parts of Asia have modernized, traditional beliefs in magical power are not uniformly and vociferously disparaged. The process of disenchantment in Western modernity is not paralleled by a systematic decline in Asian cultural concerns with magic and charisma. In a sense, Asian cultures are still embedded in an enchanted universe in which symbolic interaction with the world of magic has not fully abated.[12] Disenchantment is, therefore, an unwieldy goal of modernization in Asia, problematizing the assumption that the attenuation of magic is a *sine qua non* of modernity. On the contrary, uninhibited access to popular folk healers and shamans makes re-enchantment a redundant term in many modern Asian societies.

Yet, Asian societies are not shielded from the globalizing effects of the sign originating in the West. The impact of the sign in Asia can be found in the economic and cultural domains.[13] Signs in these domains are readily transformed into symbols of prestige to signify the status of modernization. For example, proliferating signs in marketing, advertising, mass communications and electronic technologies are treated in many modernizing Asian societies as symbols of advanced economic and cultural development. Although signs are products of an elaborate system of consumption and codification, they are not immune to manipulation by various groups and individuals as symbols for advancing their interests. On the other hand, it is ironic that some Asian religions have become symbolic sources for sign-driven re-enchantment in the West. The examples of New Age tantrism and Falungong discussed in previous chapters demonstrate the absorption of Hindu and Taoist symbols by the Western market of new religious signs.

The new millennium has ushered in social processes that are leading to re-enchantment in the West and dynamic eclecticism in Asia. The immanence of charisma has perforated the screen of world mastery to challenge the Enlightenment hegemony of the rational self. The meaning of Enlightenment can no longer be taken at face value. The advent of the sign suggests new developments that spell the end of Enlightenment.

The End of Enlightenment

The symbols that we grew up with have become the signs that we will die by. Modernization in the West has reached a point of reversibility. The symbols of rational progress that guided the activities of the last few centuries seem to have outlived their utility. Religious beliefs and actions under those symbols have turned individual salvation into a quest for the sovereignty of the self. Now the sign has taken over, and religious quests have become parodies of packaged ecstasy. The symbolic underpinnings of the Western Enlightenment have fractured under the weight of its own ambitions. The emergence of a sign-driven world lays bare the fragility of all symbolic undertakings.

The Western Enlightenment opened the world to unlimited inquiry. Empirical knowledge derived from this inquiry became the symbolic canopy for institutionalizing the meaning of progress and world mastery. The symbol could not be torn asunder because it performed the unenviable task of holding together the relationship between the self of knowing and the myriad objects that needed to be known. The self became the fulcrum for the representation of all knowledge. God could not be cajoled to be the ultimate symbol of truth. This symbol was assigned to the pursuits of the Enlightenment.

In the age of the sign, the symbol takes a back seat in the manufacture of meaning. The implosion of the signifier and signified in the sign implies that symbolic representation today is, at best, an inconvenient residue of bourgeois privilege or, at worst, a desperate return to the fading world of disenchanted meanings. In religion, the sign does not pretend to make holy the notion of salvation. It declines to represent acts of religiosity with the meaning of truth. Neither does it trap divinity in unending exegesis of religious experience. The power of the sign compels the self to enter into religious experiences without the compunction to activate symbolic interpretation. Consequently, the self becomes its own gateway to other signs that may, in the long run, have an attenuating effect on subjective consciousness.

Re-enchantment under the sign, therefore, implies the end of Enlightenment because the symbols of disenchantment, so vital to the dissemination of truth, are now in disarray and cannot unilaterally maintain the world as a repository of candid knowledge for the development of the self. The self, wishing to be released from the clutches of world mastery, seeks loopholes in symbolic interaction to disconnect from the burden of institutionalizing end-states.[14] These loopholes are the de-differentiating moments of symbolic activity that transform self-autonomy into unmediated charismatic experience. In a sense, fundamentalism is mistakenly treated as an extreme effort to institutionalize end-states, when it is nothing more than an Arcadian effort to actualize the loopholes of de-differentiating experiences. To a certain extent, fundamentalists recognize the power of the sign in scriptural literalism that makes equivalent the experiences of everyday life and those of the hereafter. But they fail to reclaim the symbols of eschatology as the hidden signs of charisma. This has principally been the accomplishment of the New Age movement.

What has made the New Age movement a significant indicator of post-symbolic religious activities is its vibrant proliferation of signs that collapse the exoteric and esoteric realms of knowledge. The New Age movement is largely a Western phenomenon with roots in romanticism and the youth rebellion of the 1960s. It provides an excellent example of religious transformation that accentuates the immanence of charisma. The sense of the holy and magical is no longer confined to the religious sphere, but revealed in various aspects of everyday life. The New Age seeker can tap into different religious traditions to excavate holistic beliefs and practices. Elements of these traditions are incorporated into marketable new religions. New Age shamans, too, have contributed to the popularization of holistic beliefs and practices. They do not make explicit distinctions between esoteric knowledge and knowledge for negotiating the world. In short, New Age shamans are pioneering methods for inducing spiritual experiences that minimize the need for symbolic representation. The experience itself is the sign for verifying the simultaneity of all knowledge. Thus, re-enchantment in the New Age poses a threat to Enlightenment because it opens the way to a type of antinomianism where knowledge is the power of the heart standing above the symbolic relations of truth.

Would re-enchantment also redefine the meaning of esoteric knowledge? If re-enchantment suggests that the world is perceived without the lenses of differentiation, then esoteric knowledge would not be grasped simply as the special preserve of mystics. Rather, the exoteric and esoteric is bridged by a continuum of understanding that cuts through the compartmentalization of knowledge. The gradation from the mundane to the mystical is governed by shifts in perspective that can occur through shamanic training, and various forms of meditation now available to the public. Re-enchantment in the New Age deconstructs esotericism as a play of signs that could lead to the realization of the 'emptiness' of all identities.

A reconsideration of the continuum between exoteric and esoteric knowledge suggests that religion in the age of the sign may no longer depend on a subject-driven quest for salvation. Such a continuum can empower a different experience of religion that elevates the immanence of charisma over symbolic interaction. The notion of Enlightenment would be considered otiose because the self ceases its delight in dualistic dalliance. Religion may evolve into an emporium of sign-filled fulfilment in which no individual can unilaterally claim subjective privilege on the road to salvation. Each individual is absorbed by the sign to embrace the vastness of existential interdependency instead of dwelling on the intricacies of teleological finality. Religion is shattered as symbolic culture comes under the power of the sign.

Notes

1 Jean Baudrillard (1990), *Cool Memories*, London: Verso, p.4.
2 Max Weber (1946), *From Max Weber: Essays in Sociology*, New York: Oxford University Press, pp.282–3.
3 Keith Thomas (1973), *Religion and the Decline of Magic*, Harmondsworth: Penguin, p.182.
4 Weber, *From Max Weber, op. cit.*, p.143.
5 Ibid., p.139.
6 Many works have appeared that question the meaning and utility of science. See for example, Karen Knorr-Cetina and Michael Mulkay (eds) (1983), *Science Observed: Perspectives on the Social Study of Science*, London: Sage; Bruno Latour and Steve Woolgar (1986), *Laboratory Life: The Construction of Scientific Facts*, Princeton, NJ: Princeton University Press; Ziauddin Sardar (ed.) (1988), *The Revenge of Athena: Science, Exploitation and the Third World*, London: Mansell.
7 See Howard Rhinegold (1992), *Virtual Reality*, New York: Simon and Schuster.
8 For a comparison of these movements, see Catherine Wessinger (2000), *How the Millennium Comes Violently: From Jonestown to Heaven's Gate*, New York: Seven Bridges Press.

9 For Western treatment of Buddhist approaches to emptiness, see C.W. Huntington, Jr (1989), *The Emptiness of Emptiness*, Honolulu, HI: University of Hawaii Press; Jeffrey Hopkins (1995), *Emptiness Yoga*, Ithaca, NY: Snow Lion.

10 J.J. Clarke (1997), *Oriental Enlightenment: The Encounter Between Asian and Western Thought*. London: Routledge, p.213.

11 Ibid., p.221.

12 For a sample of works dealing with this phenomenon, see Alan J.A. Elliott (1964), *Chinese Spirit-Medium Cults in Singapore*, Singapore: Donald Moore; Richard W. Lieban (1967), *Cebuano Sorcery: Malign Magic in the Philippines*, Berkeley, CA: University of California Press; Niels Mulder (1978), *Mysticism and Everyday Life in Contemporary Java,* Singapore: Singapore University Press; Winston Davis (1980), *Dojo: Magic and Exorcism in Modern Japan*, Stanford, CA: Stanford University Press.

13 The McDonaldization of Asian societies could be seen as an example of the creeping effect of the sign in Asia. See, for example, James Watson (ed.) (1997), *Golden Arches East: McDonald's in East Asia*, Stanford, CA: Stanford University Press.

14 Hence, the term 'postmodern' suggests that modernity is not an end-state since one could overcome and evolve beyond it.

Bibliography

Abercrombie, Nicholas and Urry, John (1983), *Capital, Labour and the Middle Classes*, London: Allen and Unwin.

Ackerman, Susan E. (2001), 'Divine Contracts: Chinese New Religions and Shamanic Movements in Contemporary Malaysia', *Journal of Contemporary Religion*, 16(3), pp.293–311.

Ahady, Anwar-ul-Haq (1992), 'The Decline of Islamic Fundamentalism', *Journal of Asian and African Studies*, 27, pp.229–43.

Ahmed, Akbar S. (1988), *Discovering Islam*, London: Routledge.

Albanese, Catherine L. (1993), 'Fisher Kings and Public Places: The Old New Age in the 1990s', *Annals of the American Academy of Political and Social Science*, 527, pp.131–43.

Aran, Gideon (1991), 'Jewish Zionist Fundamentalism: The Bloc of the Faithful in Israel (Gush Emunim)', in M.E. Marty and R.S. Appleby (eds), *Fundamentalisms Observed*, Chicago: University of Chicago Press.

Asad, Talal (1997), 'Europe Against Islam: Islam in Europe', *The Muslim World*, 87, pp.183–95.

Bainbridge, William S. (1997), *The Sociology of Religious Movements*, London: Routledge.

Batchelor, Stephen (1994), *The Awakening of the West: The Encounter of Buddhism and Western Culture*, Berkeley, CA: Parallax Press.

Baudrillard, Jean (1983), *Simulations*, New York: Semiotext(e).

Baudrillard, Jean (1990a), *Fatal Strategies*, New York: Semiotext(e).

Baudrillard, Jean (1990b), *Cool Memories*, London: Verso.

Baudrillard, Jean (1993), *Symbolic Exchange and Death*, London: Sage.

Baudrillard, Jean (1996), *The System of Objects*, London: Verso.

Bauman, Zygmunt (1989), *Modernity and the Holocaust*, Cambridge: Polity Press.

Bauman, Zygmunt (1990), 'Modernity and Ambivalence', in M. Featherstone (ed.), *Global Culture*, London: Sage.

Baumann, Martin (1997), 'The Dharma Has Come West: A Survey of Recent Studies and Sources', *Journal of Buddhist Ethics*, 4, pp.194–211.

Beck, Ulrich (1992), *Risk Society*, London: Sage.

Beck, Ulrich, Giddens, Anthony and Lash, Scott (1994), *Reflexive Modernization*, Cambridge: Polity Press.

Beckford, James A. (1985), *Cult Controversies*, London: Tavistock.

Beckford, James A. (1992), *Religion and Advanced Industrial Society*, London: Routledge.

Berger, Peter (1969), *The Sacred Canopy*, New York: Anchor Books.
Berman, Marshall (1983), *All That is Solid Melts into Air*, London: Verso.
Bishop, Peter (1993), *Dreams of Power: Tibetan Buddhism and the Western Imagination*, Madison, NJ: Fairleigh Dickinson University Press.
Blumenberg, Hans (1983), *The Legitimation of the Modern Age*, Cambridge, MA: MIT Press.
Bowring, Finn (1996), 'A Lifeworld Without a Subject: Habermas and the Pathologies of Modernity', *Telos*, 106, pp.77–104.
Bruce, Steve (ed.) (1992), *Religion and Modernization*, Oxford: Clarendon Press.
Camic, Charles (1980), 'Charisma: Its Varieties, Preconditions, and Consequences', *Sociological Inquiry*, 50, pp.5–23.
Campbell, Colin (1987), *The Romantic Ethic and the Spirit of Consumerism*, Oxford: Blackwell.
Caplan, Lionel (ed.) (1987), *Studies in Religious Fundamentalism*, Albany, NY: SUNY Press.
Caplow, Theodore (1985), 'Contrasting Trends in European and American Religion', *Sociological Analysis*, 46, pp.101–8.
Carter, Lewis (1990), *Charisma and Control in Rajneeshpuram*, New York: Cambridge University Press.
Castaneda, Carlos (1968), *The Teachings of Don Juan.*, New York: Ballantine Books.
Castaneda, Carlos (1971), *A Separate Reality*, New York: Simon and Schuster.
Castaneda, Carlos (1972), *Journey to Ixtlan*, New York: Simon and Schuster.
Castaneda, Carlos (1974), *Tales of Power*, New York: Simon and Schuster.
Castaneda, Carlos (1977), *The Second Ring of Power*, New York: Simon and Schuster.
Castaneda, Carlos (1981), *The Eagle's Gift*, New York: Simon and Schuster.
Castaneda, Carlos (1984), *The Fire From Within*, New York: Simon and Schuster.
Castaneda, Carlos (1991), *The Power of Silence*, New York: Pocket Books.
Castaneda, Carlos (1994), *The Art of Dreaming*, New York: Harper.
Castaneda, Carlos (1998a), *The Wheel of Time*, Los Angeles: Eidolona Press.
Castaneda, Carlos (1998b), *Magical Passes*, New York: HarperCollins.
Castaneda, Carlos (1998c), *The Active Side of Infinity*, New York: HarperCollins.
Cell, Charles P. (1974), 'Charismatic Heads of State: The Social Context', *Behavioral Science Research*, 9, pp.255–305.
Chaves, Mark (1994), 'Secularization as Declining Religious Authority', *Social Forces*, 72, pp.749–74.
Christensen, Jerome (1994), 'The Romantic Movement at the End of History', *Critical Inquiry*, 20, pp.452–76.
Chu, J.J. (1996), 'Taiwan: A Fragmented Middle Class in the Making', in R. Robison and D. Goodman (eds), *The New Rich in Asia*, London: Routledge.

Clarke, J.J. (1997), *Oriental Enlightenment: The Encounter Between Asian and Western Thought*, London: Routledge.

Davis, Winston (1980), *Dojo: Magic and Exorcism in Modern Japan*, Stanford, CA: Stanford University Press.

Davis, Winston (1991), 'Fundamentalism in Japan: Religious and Political', in M.E. Marty and R.S. Appleby (eds), *Fundamentalisms Observed*, Chicago: University of Chicago Press.

De Mille, Richard (1976), *Castaneda's Journey*, Santa Barbara, CA: Capra Press.

De Mille, Richard (1980), *The Don Juan Papers*, Santa Barbara, CA: Ross Erickson.

Denny, Frederick M. (1985), 'Islam: Qur'an and Hadith', in F.M. Denny and R.L. Taylor (eds), *The Holy Book in Comparative Perspective*. Columbia, SC: University of South Carolina Press.

Dieter-Evers, Hans (ed.) (1993), 'Religious Revivalism in Southeast Asia', Special issue of *Sojourn: Social Issues in Southeast Asia*, 8(1), pp.1–218.

Dobbelaere, Karel (1981), 'Secularization: A Multi-Dimensional Concept', *Current Sociology*, 29, pp.1–216.

Dobkin de Rios, Marlene (1972), *Visionary Vine*, San Francisco: Chandler.

Domhoff, G. William (1985), *The Mystique of Dreams*, Berkeley, CA: University of California Press.

Douglas, Mary (1994), *Risk and Blame*, London: Routledge.

Drolma, Dawa Delog (1995), *Delog: Journey to Realms Beyond Death*, Junction City, CA: Padma Publishing.

Dusenbery, Verne A. (1989), 'Of Singh Sabhas, Siri Singh Sahibs, and Sikh Scholars: Sikh Discourse From North America in the 1970s', in N.G. Barrier and V.A. Dusenbery (eds), *The Sikh Diaspora*, Delhi: Chanakya Publications.

Eliade, Mircea (1964), *Shamanism: Archaic Techniques of Ecstasy*. Princeton, NJ: Princeton University Press.

Eliade, Mircea (1969), *Yoga: Immortality and Freedom*, Princeton, NJ: Princeton University Press.

Elliott, Alan J.A. (1964), *Chinese Spirit-Medium Cults in Singapore*, Singapore: Donald Moore.

Ellwood, Robert S., Jr (1973), *Religious and Spiritual Groups in Modern America*, Englewood Cliffs, NJ: Prentice Hall.

Ellwood, Robert S., Jr (1979), *Alternative Altars: Unconventional and Eastern Spirituality in America*, Chicago: University of Chicago Press.

Esposito, John L. (1992), *The Islamic Threat: Myth or Reality?*, New York: Oxford University Press.

Fabian, Johannes (1966), 'Dreams and Charisma: "Theories of Dreams" in the Jamaa-Movement (Congo)', *Anthropos*, 61, pp.544–60.

Faraday, Ann (1974), *Dream Power*, London: Pan.

Faraday, Ann (1976), *The Dream Game*, Harmondsworth: Penguin.

Featherstone, Mike (1991), *Consumer Culture and Postmodernism*, London: Sage.

Fenn, Richard K. (1978), *Toward a Theory of Secularization*, Storrs, CN: Society for the Scientific Study of Religion.

Fields, Rick (1992), *How the Swans Came to the Lake: A Narrative History of Buddhism in America*, Boston: Shambala.

Foster, Hal (ed.) (1985), *Postmodern Culture*, London: Pluto Press.

Foucault, Michel (1977), *Discipline and Punish*, Harmondsworth: Penguin.

Freud, Sigmund (1954), *The Interpretation of Dreams*, London: Allen and Unwin.

Freund, Julian (1969), *The Sociology of Max Weber*, Harmondsworth: Penguin.

Fukuyama, Francis (1992), *The End of History and the Last Man*, New York: Free Press.

Garfield, Patricia (1974), *Creative Dreaming*, New York: Ballantine Books.

Gay, Peter (1977), *The Enlightenment*, 2 vols, New York: Norton.

Giddens, Anthony (1990), *The Consequences of Modernity*, Cambridge: Polity Press.

Giddens, Anthony (1991), *Modernity and Self-Identity*, Cambridge: Polity Press.

Giddens, Anthony (1994), *Beyond Left and Right*, Cambridge: Polity Press.

Gilbert, Alan D. (1980), *The Making of Post-Christian Britain*, London: Longman.

Gitlin, Todd (1993), *The Sixties: Years of Hope, Days of Rage*, New York: Bantam Books.

Glassman, Ronald (1975), 'Legitimacy and Manufactured Charisma', *Social Research*, 42, pp.615–36.

Gold, Daniel (1991), 'Organized Hinduisms: From Vedic Truth to Hindu Nation', in M.E. Marty and R.S. Appleby (eds), *Fundamentalisms Observed*, Chicago: University of Chicago Press.

Gottdiener, Mark (1985), 'Hegemony and Mass Culture: A Socio-Semiotic Approach', *American Journal of Sociology*, 90, pp.979–1001.

Greeley, Andrew W. (1974), *Ecstasy: A Way of Knowing*, Englewood Cliffs, NJ: Prentice Hall.

Green, Celia E. (1968), *Lucid Dreams*, London: Hamish Hamilton.

Green, Celia E. and McCreery, Charles (1994), *Lucid Dreaming*, London: Routledge.

Gronow, Jukka (1988), 'The Element of Irrationality: Max Weber's Diagnosis of Modern Culture', *Acta Sociologica*, 31, pp.319–31

Groth, Alexander J. (1971), *Major Ideologies*, New York: Wiley.

Habermas, Jürgen (1984), *The Theory of Communicative Action*, Vol. 1, Boston: Beacon.

Habermas, Jürgen (1987a), *The Theory of Communicative Action*, Vol. 2, Boston: Beacon.

Habermas, Jürgen (1987b), *The Philosophical Discourse of Modernity*, Cambridge, MA: MIT Press.

Hadden, Jeffrey K. (1987), 'Toward Desacralizing Secularization Theory', *Social Forces*, 65, pp.587–611.

Hadden, Jeffrey K. and Shupe, Anson (eds) (1989), *Secularization and Fundamentalism Reconsidered*, New York: Paragon House.

Haley, Peter D. (1980), 'The Idea of Charismatic Authority: From Theology to Sociology', unpublished Ph.D. dissertation, University of Pennsylvania.

Harary, Keith and Weintraub, Pamela (1989), *Lucid Dreaming in 30 Days*, New York: St. Martin's Press.

Harner, Michael (ed.) (1973), *Hallucinogens and Shamanism*, New York: Oxford University Press.

Harner, Michael (1980), *The Way of the Shaman*, New York: Harper and Row.

Harvey, David (1989), *The Condition of Postmodernity*, Oxford: Blackwell.

Heelas, Paul (1996), *The New Age Movement*, London: Routledge.

Hewison, Kevin (1996), 'Emerging Social Forces in Thailand: New Political and Economic Roles', in R. Robison and D. Goodman (eds), *The New Rich in Asia*, London: Routledge.

Hill, Michael (1973), *A Sociology of Religion*, London: Heinemann.

Hooykaas, R. (1972), *Religion and the Rise of Modern Science*, Edinburgh: Scottish Academic Press.

Hopkins, Jeffrey (1995), *Emptiness Yoga*, Ithaca, NY: Snow Lion.

Horkheimer, Max and Adorno, Theodor W. (1973), *Dialectic of Enlightenment*, London: Allen Lane.

Hughes, H. Stuart (1961), *Consciousness and Society*, New York: Vintage.

Huntington, C.W., Jr. (1989), *The Emptiness of Emptiness*, Honolulu, HI: University of Hawaii Press.

Huntington, Samuel (1996), *The Clash of Civilizations and the Remaking of World Order*, New York: Simon and Schuster.

Jameson, Fredric (1991), *Postmodernism or the Cultural Logic of Late Capitalism*, Durham, NC: Duke University Press.

Jones, Howard M. (1974), *Revolution and Romanticism*, Cambridge, MA: Belknap Press.

Jordan, David K. and Overmeyer, Daniel L. (1986), *The Flying Phoenix: Aspects of Chinese Sectarianism in Taiwan*, Princeton, NJ: Princeton University Press.

Juergensmeyer, Mark (1993), *The New Cold War: Religious Nationalism Confronts the State*, Berkeley, MA: University of California Press.

Jung, Carl G. (1974), *Dreams*, Princeton, NJ: Princeton University Press.

Kaplan, Lawrence (ed.) (1992), *Fundamentalism in Comparative Perspective*, Amherst, MA: University of Massachusetts Press.

Kepel, Gilles (1994), *The Revenge of God: The Resurgence of Islam, Christianity and Judaism in the Modern World*, Cambridge: Polity Press.

Kim, Kwang-Ok (1994), 'Rituals of Resistance: The Manipulation of Shamanism in Contemporary Korea', in C. Keyes, L. Kendall and H.Hardacre (eds), *Asian Visions of Authority: Religion and the Modern States of East and Southeast Asia*, Honolulu, HI: University of Hawaii Press.

Klapp, Orrin E. (1969), *Collective Search for Identity*, New York: Holt, Rinehart and Winston.

Knorr-Cetina, Karen and Michael Mulkay (eds) (1983), *Science Observed: Perspectives on the Social Study of Science*, London: Sage.

LaBerge, Stephen (1985), *Lucid Dreaming*, New York: Ballantine Books.

LaBerge, Stephen and Rhinegold, Howard (1990), *Exploring the World of Lucid Dreaming*, New York: Ballantine Books.

LaBerge, Stephen and DeGracia, Donald J. (2000), 'Varieties of Lucid Dreaming', in K.G. Kunzendorf and B. Wallace (eds), *Individual Differences in Conscious Experience*, Amsterdam: John Benjamins.

Lanternari, Vittorio (1963), *The Religions of the Oppressed*, New York: Alfred Knopf.

Lanternari, Vittorio (1975), 'Dreams as Charismatic Significants: Their Bearing on the Rise of New Religious Movements', in T.R. Williams (ed.), *Psychological Anthropology*, The Hague: Mouton.

Lash, Scott (1990), *Sociology of Postmodernism*, London: Routledge.

Latour, Bruno and Woolgar, Steve (1986), *Laboratory Life: The Construction of Scientific Facts*, Princeton, NJ: Princeton University Press.

Lawrence, Bruce B. (1995), *Defenders of God: The Fundamentalist Revolt Against the Modern Age*, Columbia, SC: University of South Carolina Press.

Leary, Timothy (1970), *The Politics of Ecstasy*, London: Paladin.

Lee, Raymond L.M. and Ackerman, Susan E. (1997), *Sacred Tensions: Modernity and Religious Transformation in Malaysia*, Columbia, SC: University of South Carolina Press.

Lester, Robert C. (1985), 'Hinduism: Veda and Sacred Texts', in F.M. Denny and R.L. Taylor (eds), *The Holy Book in Comparative Perspective*, Columbia, SC: University of South Carolina Press.

Levin, Donald (1981), 'Rationality and Freedom: Weber and Beyond', *Sociological Inquiry*, 51, pp.5–25.

Lewis, James and Melton, Gordon (eds) (1992), *Perspectives on the New Age*, Albany, NY: SUNY Press.

Lieban, Richard W. (1967), *Cebuano Sorcery: Malign Magic in the Philippines*, Berkeley, CA: University of California Press.

Lopez, Donald S., Jr. (1998), *Prisoners of Shangri-La: Tibetan Buddhism and the West*, Chicago: University of Chicago Press.

Löwith, Karl (1949), *Meaning in History*, Chicago: University of Chicago Press.

Löwy, Michael (1996), *The War of Gods: Religion and Politics in Latin America*, London: Verso.

Luckmann, Thomas (1967), *The Invisible Religion*, London: Macmillan.
Luhmann, Niklas (1993), *Risk: A Sociological Theory*, New York: Aldine de Gruyter.
Lukács, Georg (1971), *History and Class Consciousness*, Cambridge, MA: MIT Press.
McCreery, Charles (1973), *Psychical Phenomena and the Physical World*, London: Hamish Hamilton.
McFarland, H. Neill (1967), *The Rush Hour of the Gods*, New York: Harper and Row.
Mack, John E. (1974), *Nightmares and Human Conflict*, Boston: Houghton Mifflin.
Mackenzie, Vicki (1988), *Reincarnation: The Boy Lama*. London: Bloomsbury.
Mackenzie, Vicki (1996), *Reborn in the West: The Reincarnation Masters*, New York: Marlowe.
Madan, T.N. (1991),'The Double-Edged Sword: Fundamentalism and the Sikh Religious Tradition', in M.E. Marty and R.S. Appleby (eds), *Fundamentalisms Observed*, Chicago: University of Chicago Press.
Manzoor, S. Parvez (1991), 'The Future of Muslim Politics: Critique of the 'Fundamentalist' Theory of the Islamic State', *Futures*, 23, pp.289–301.
Marsden, George M. (1980), *Fundamentalism and American Culture*, New York: Oxford University Press.
Martin, David (1978a), *A General Theory of Secularization*, Oxford: Blackwell.
Martin, David (1978b), *The Dilemmas of Contemporary Religion*, Oxford: Blackwell.
Martin, David (1990), *Tongues of Fire: The Explosion of Protestantism in Latin America*, Oxford: Blackwell.
Martin, Richard C. (1994), 'Review of *Fundamentalisms Observed* and *Fundamentalism in Comparative Perspective*', *History of Religions*, 34, pp.194–6.
Marty, Martin E. (1984), 'Fundamentalism as a Social Phenomenon', in G.M. Marsden (ed.), *Evangelicalism and Modern America*, Grand Rapids, MI: Eerdmans.
Marty, Martin E. and R. Scott Appleby (1991), 'Conclusion: An Interim Report on a Hypothetical Family', in M.E. Marty and R.S. Appleby (eds), *Fundamentalisms Observed*, Chicago: University of Chicago Press.
Marty, Martin E. and Appleby, R. Scott (eds) (1991), *Fundamentalisms Observed*, Chicago: University of Chicago Press.
Marty, Martin E. and Appleby, R. Scott (eds) (1992), *Fundamentalisms and Society*, Chicago: University of Chicago Press.
Marty, Martin E. and Appleby, R. Scott (eds) (1993), *Fundamentalisms and the State*, Chicago: University of Chicago Press.
Marty, Martin E. and Appleby, R. Scott (eds) (1994), *Accounting for Fundamentalisms*, Chicago: University of Chicago Press.

Marty, Martin E. and Appleby, R. Scott (eds) (1995), *Fundamentalisms Comprehended*, Chicago: University of Chicago Press.

Melton, Gordon (1990), *New Age Encyclopedia*, Detroit, MI: Gale Research.

Mernissi, Fatima (1992), *Islam and Democracy*, Reading, MA: Addison-Wesley.

Metraux, Daniel A. (1995), 'Religious Terrorism in Japan', *Asian Survey*, 35, pp.1140–54.

Michael, Franz (1982), *Rule by Incarnation: Tibetan Buddhism and Its Role in Society and State*, Boulder, CO: Westview Press.

Moss, Robert (1996), *Conscious Dreaming*, New York: Crown Publishing Group.

Mulder, Niels (1978), *Mysticism and Everyday Life in Contemporary Java*, Singapore: Singapore University Press.

Murchland, Bernard (1970), *The Age of Alienation*, New York: Random House.

Myerhoff, Barbara (1974), *Peyote Hunt*, Ithaca, NY: Cornell University Press.

Noda, Nobuo (1996), 'Apocalyptic Cults and Japanese Religiosity', *Japan Review of International Affairs*, 10, pp.116–27.

Noel, Daniel (ed.) (1976), *Seeing Castaneda*, New York: Putnam.

Norbu, Namkhai C. (1992), *Dream Yoga and the Practice of Natural Light*, Ithaca, NY: Snow Lion.

Norbu, Namkhai C. (1993), *The Crystal and the Way of Light*, New York: Arkana.

Norbu, Namkhai C. (1996), *Dzogchen: The Self-Perfected State*, Ithaca, NY: Snow Lion.

Oberoi, Harjot (1993), 'Sikh Fundamentalism: Translating History into Theory', in M.E. Marty and R.S. Appleby (eds), *Fundamentalisms and the State*, Chicago: University of Chicago Press.

Overmyer, Daniel L. (1981), 'Alternatives: Popular Religious Sects in Chinese Society', *Modern China*, 7(2), pp.153–90.

Perinbayanagam, R.S. (1971), 'The Dialectics of Charisma', *Sociological Quarterly*, 12, pp.387–402.

Peters, Larry and Price-Williams, Douglass (1980), 'Towards an Experiential Analysis of Shamanism', *American Ethnologist*, 7, pp.397–418.

Pipes, Daniel (1989), 'Fundamentalist Muslims in World Politics', in J.K. Hadden and A. Shupe (eds), *Secularization and Fundamentalism Reconsidered*, New York: Paragon House.

Rahman, Fazlur (1981), 'Roots of Islamic Neo-Fundamentalism', in R.H. Stoddard, D.C. Cuthall and M.W. Sullivan (eds), *Change and the Muslim World*, Syracuse, NY: Syracuse University Press.

Reader, Ian (1991), *Religion in Contemporary Japan*, London: Macmillan.

Rhinegold, Howard (1992), *Virtual Reality*, New York: Simon and Schuster.

Ritzer, George (1995), *The McDonaldization of Society*, Thousand Oaks, CA: Sage.

Robbins, Thomas (1988), 'Cults, Converts, and Charisma: The Sociology of New Religious Movements', *Current Sociology*, 36 (1), pp.1–256.

Robison, Richard and Goodman, David (eds) (1996), *The New Rich in Asia*, London: Routledge.

Roff, William R. (1967), *The Origins of Malay Nationalism*, New Haven, CN: Yale University Press.

Rose, Margaret A. (1991), *The Post-Modern and the Post-Industrial*, Cambridge: Cambridge University Press.

Russell, Bertrand (1961), *History of Western Philosophy*, London: Allen and Unwin.

Saiedi, Nader (1986), 'What is Islamic Fundamentalism?', in J.K. Hadden and A. Shupe (eds), *Prophetic Religions and Politics*, New York: Paragon House.

Samuel, Geoffrey (1995), *Civilized Shamans: Buddhism in Tibetan Societies*, Washington DC: Smithsonian Institution.

Sardar, Ziauddin (ed.) (1988), *The Revenge of Athena*, London: Mansell.

Sarup, Madan (1993), *An Introductory Guide to Post-Structuralism and Postmodernism*, Athens, GA: University of Georgia Press.

Satha-Anand, Suwanna (1990), 'Religious Movements in Contemporary Thailand', *Asian Survey*, 30, pp.395–408.

Seidman, Steven (1994), *Contested Knowledge*, Oxford: Blackwell.

Shalin, Dmitri (1986), 'Romanticism and the Rise of Sociological Hermeneutics', *Social Research*, 53, pp.77–123.

Sharma, Arvind (1988), 'The Sikh Crisis in India: A Question of Identity', in A. Shupe and J.K. Hadden (eds), *The Politics of Religion and Social Change*, New York: Paragon House.

Shils, Edward (1965), 'Charisma, Order, and Status', *American Sociological Review*, 30, pp.199–213.

Shiner, Larry (1967), 'The Concept of Secularization in Empirical Research', *Journal for the Scientific Study of Religion*, 6, pp.202–20.

Shupe, Anson and Bromley, David G. (1980), *The New Vigilantes*, Beverly Hills, CA: Sage.

Shupe, Anson and Hadden, Jeffrey K. (1989), 'Is There Such a Thing as Global Fundamentalism?', in J.K. Hadden and A. Shupe (eds), *Secularization and Fundamentalism Reconsidered*, New York: Paragon House.

Sica, Alan (1988), *Weber, Irrationality, and Social Order*, Berkeley, CA: University of California Press.

Spencer, Martin E. (1973), 'What is Charisma?', *British Journal of Sociology*, 24, pp.341–54.

Stark, Rodney (1997), *The Rise of Christianity*, San Francisco: HarperCollins.

Stark, Rodney and Bainbridge, William S. (1985), *The Future of Religion*, Berkeley, CA: University of California Press.

Stephen, Michelle (1982), 'Dreaming is Another Power: The Social Significance of Dreams Among the Mekeo of Papua New Guinea', *Oceania*, 53(2), pp.106–22.

Stewart, Kilton (1972), 'Dream Theory in Malaya', in C.T. Tart (ed.), *Altered States of Consciousness*, New York: Anchor Books.

Swatos, William H., Jr. (1981), 'The Disenchantment of Charisma: A Weberian Assessment of Revolution in a Rationalized World', *Sociological Analysis*, 42, pp.119–36.

Swearer, Donald K. (1991), 'Fundamentalistic Movements in Theravada Buddhism', in M.E. Marty and R.S. Appleby (eds), *Fundamentalisms Observed*, Chicago: University of Chicago Press.

Tamney, Joseph B. (1992), *American Society in the Buddhist Mirror*, New York: Garland.

Tapp, Nicholas (1993), "Karma and Cosmology: Anthropology and Religion', in G. Evans (ed.), *Asia's Cultural Mosaic*, New York: Prentice Hall.

Tester, Keith (1993), *The Life and Times of Post-Modernity*, London: Routledge.

Thomas, Keith (1973), *Religion and the Decline of Magic*, Harmondsworth: Penguin.

Tibi, Bassam (1988), *The Crisis of Modern Islam*, Salt Lake City, UT: University of Utah Press.

Tiryakian, Edward A. (1974), 'Toward the Sociology of Esoteric Culture', in E.A. Tiryakian (ed.), *On the Margin of the Visible: Sociology, the Esoteric, and the Occult*, New York: Wiley.

Tiryakian, Edward A. (1992), 'Dialectics of Modernity: Reenchantment and Dedifferentiation as Counter-processes', in H. Haferkamp and N.J. Smelser (eds), *Social Change and Modernity*, Berkeley, CA: University of California Press.

Trungpa, Chöygam (1991), *Orderly Chaos: The Mandala Principle*, Boston: Shambala.

Tucci, Giuseppe (1961), *The Theory and Practice of the Mandala*, London: Rider.

Urban, Hugh B. (2000), 'The Cult of Ecstasy: Tantrism, the New Age, and the Spiritual Logic of Late Capitalism', *History of Religions*, 39, pp.268–304.

Van Eeden, Frederik (1972), 'A Study of Dreams', in C.T. Tart (ed.), *Altered States of Consciousness*, New York: Anchor Books.

Voll, John O. (1991), 'Fundamentalism in the Sunni Arab World: Egypt and the Sudan', in M.E. Marty and R.S. Appleby (eds), *Fundamentalisms Observed*, Chicago: University of Chicago Press.

Wakeman, Frederick, Jr (1977), 'Rebellion and Revolution: The Study of Popular Movements in Chinese History', *Journal of Asian Studies*, 36(2), pp.1–37.

Wallerstein, Immanuel (1983), *World System and Capitalist Civilization*, London: Verso.

Wallis, Roy (1984), *The Elementary Forms of the New Religious Life*, London: Routledge.
Watson, James (ed.) (1997), *Golden Arches East: McDonald's in East Asia*, Stanford, CA: Stanford University Press.
Wessinger, Catherine (2000), *How the Millennium Comes Violently: From Jonestown to Heaven's Gate*, New York: Seven Bridges Press.
Williams, Raymond (1971), *Culture and Society 1780-1950*, Harmondsworth: Penguin.
Weber, Max (1946), 'Science as a Vocation', in *From Max Weber: Essays in Sociology*, New York: Oxford University Press.
Weber, Max (1968), *Economy and Society*, New York: Bedminster Press
Wilson, Bryan (1966), *Religion in Secular Society*, Harmondsworth: Penguin.
Wilson, Bryan (1973), *Magic and the Millennium*, New York: Harper and Row.
Wilson, Bryan (1976), *Contemporary Transformations of Religion*, Oxford: Clarendon Press.
Wuthnow, Robert (1978), *Experimentation in American Religion*, Berkeley, CA: University of California Press.
Yeshe, Lama Thubten (1991), *Transference of Consciousness at the Time of Death*, Boston: Wisdom Publications.
York, Michael (1995), *The Emerging Network: A Sociology of New Age and New Religious Movements*, Lanham, MD: Rowman and Littlefield.
Zijderveld, Anton C. (1970), *The Abstract Society*, London: Allen Lane.

Index